# Just O...
*Elizabe...*

C000254000

First published in 2011 by Elizabeth Sandie, North Parade, York

© 2011 Elizabeth Sandie and Contributors

All stories were developed from original interviews. Some names and identifying details have been changed to protect the privacy of individuals.

ISBN: 978-0-9570422-0-9

All rights reserved.
No reproduction of this text without written permission.

Photographs of Will, Kildip, Karen, Patrick, Megan, Gemma, Greg and Monika's family are copyright of the respective interviewee and are used here with permission. All other photographs, unless shown otherwise, are copyright of Elizabeth Sandie.

Typesetting and Production: Route Publishing
Cover Design: GOLDEN

Printed by CPI Antony Rowe

Commissioned by Chrysalis Arts as part of the Extending Practice/ Celebrating Place project.

This project is part financed through funding made available from Business Link York and North Yorkshire legacy funds and is administered by North Yorkshire County Council, City of York Council and York and North Yorkshire Chamber of Commerce.

# Contents

*For friends and neighbours
past, present and to come.*

'What matters is that people live
The ordinary all-in-a-day's-work life of peace'
U.A. Fanthorpe, *Collected Poems 1978-2003*, Peterloo Poets, 2000


'Memory isn't fixed; it slips and slides about.
Our own views of our lives change all the time,
different at different ages.'
Doris Lessing on 'Writing Autobiography' in *Time Bites*, 2004

## Introduction: Just One Street

*North Parade 1995-2011: a new life and a new millennium*

I came to live in this terrace not far outside York's City walls sixteen years ago and as I got to know my neighbours I was struck by what varied backgrounds they came from, what different worlds of work they inhabited, what interesting stories they had to tell. At one end of the street was a woman who had grown up in a croft on the Isle of Skye, at the other end, one who had grown up in Bombay.

A plan gradually evolved to collate these lives in a series of snapshots. I did two pilot interviews at the end of 2008. In February 2010 a letter went through neighbours' doors asking if they would be willing to be included. The response exceeded my expectation. The interviewees, who range in age from 14 to nearly 90, include homeowners, tenants, and young workers who house-share. I have tried to capture people's individual voices and indicate their main concerns. Changing patterns of childhood, work, leisure and family life emerge.

Often national and global issues are reflected in people's narratives – a mother who survived the Russian occupation of Poland; another who helped with the Belgian Resistance; a son fighting in Afghanistan; a sibling who emigrated after the disaster of the Foot and Mouth disease; a honeymoon cut short by the Asian Tsunami; a holiday extended because of Icelandic ash; a family visit to India delayed by the Mumbai massacre; plans affected by the recession and changes in the housing market.

York is a city rich in history. The lives of the people interviewed constitute its living history. A few interviewees commute to Leeds or even London but most work in York, mainly in the service sector, in health, education, finance, information technology and tourism; there's a civil servant and a civil engineer, a photographer and a plasterer, actors, artists, musicians, people who cook in York's restaurants, work in its theatres, ring its church bells, volunteer in its historic buildings, dig for its history, run its hotels, sing in its choirs. People reflect on the way they relate to the street, the city and the surrounding countryside; they have easy access to the dales, moors and coast of rural North Yorkshire.

Above all, the interviews show the richness and diversity of York's population. I have neighbours who grew up in very different areas of England, others who grew up in very different cultures, on different continents, as well as those like me who have spent their lives in Yorkshire. *Just One Street* reflects the random chance that has brought people here and celebrates neighbourliness within this diversity.

I have prefaced this collection of stories of thirty of the street's occupants with a sketch of the early life of the street, how it came into being at the turn of the nineteenth century and the start of the Edwardian Era. I give some insights into its first occupants gleaned from census returns and other documents against which our lives at the beginning of the twenty-first century are set.

*Elizabeth Sandie, January 2011*

# The birth of a street 1895–1901

*Moving into the Edwardian Era*

The forty-three houses which comprise North Parade were built between 1895 and 1901. This street has seen the turn of two centuries, weathered two world wars, and is witnessing now its third economic recession.

It is strange looking at a map of Bootham dated 1893 and seeing no houses where this terrace and the neighbouring Queen Anne's Road now stand. There is a large proclamation DAIRY between here and the river. Bootham Terrace is clearly visible nearer the town beside the railway line which runs to Scarborough, but from there to St Peter's School to the north, are fields, paddocks, gardens. Imagine this rural scene: no hum of traffic – instead the lowing of cattle, the clopping of horses, people out working on their crofts and orchards, steam engines passing.

York was still a market town. There were regular cattle markets and a Royal Agricultural Show here in 1900. A century before that, in the early 1800s York, already a centre of communications through its road and river networks, was also a city of small-scale handicraft businesses and trades: 'there was a small wholesale drug industry, some flour-milling, printing, linen-weaving, flint glass manufacture and a small amount of confectionary making' (*York A Survey 1959*, Brit Assoc York), but this was mostly contained inside the city walls. Restrictive practices within the city meant it was slow to respond to the industrial revolution. You actually had to be a freeman of the city, or his son or apprentice, or pay £25 before you could set up a new business.

Not until these monopolies were broken in the late 1820s and the railways arrived in 1839 did things begin to change. George Hudson had persuaded Stephenson to route the Darlington-to-London line through York rather than Leeds. The carriage-building works which followed brought new workers into the city. The existence of the railways helped other industries develop. There was a huge expansion of the building trade in York towards the end of the nineteenth century, building new streets to house manual and white collar workers.

Rowntree's chocolate factory which became the city's second largest employer began in 1864. (This Quaker family who did such a lot to promote good industrial relationships and social reform hoped drinking chocolate would become the preferred beverage to alcohol which had caused so many social problems.)

The land here outside the city walls to the north of Bootham Bar, previously administered by the East Riding, had just become part of York with the City of York Extension and Improvement Act of 1884. This would increase the city's revenues and must have been seen as a development opportunity for those who had the means.

The population of York grew from almost 17,000 in 1801 to 67,000 in 1891, the year in which John Edmund Jones, a 'Gentleman of the City of York' purchased for £3,000 the land on which this and the neighbouring terrace were built. Jones, son of a Yorkshireman, but born in Melbourne in 1847, was a solicitor living in Clifton; he was one of the best amateur boxers of his day and a founder of the Albert Victor Lodge of Freemasons. The deeds of 1 North Parade show how much Jones got for his money. His purchase included, 'A Mansion House situated in Bootham near Clifton with the coach house, stable and other outbuildings, yards, garden, plantation, pleasure grounds, croft land, paddocks.'

The plot stretched from the land behind Ingrams Hospital, the almshouses on Bootham, to the footpath at the bottom of the street leading from Marygate to Clifton. This is the snicket, referred to as 'Love Lane' on these early documents, which runs past St Peter's School, the oldest in the kingdom, founded in the eighth Century and re-endowed at the time of Queen Mary in 1575. Residents today often gather there on bonfire night to see the magnificent firework display. As Guido Fawkes was one of their most famous old boys they never burn his effigy.

North Parade and Queen Anne's Road was seen as one development and referred to on plans as *Cambridge House Estate*. A footpath leads from Queen Anne's to Bootham Terrace where there is still a *Cambridge House*. It looks as if it were once part of a larger establishment; perhaps this was the Mansion referred to in the deeds.

Number 1 North Parade was first owned by the builder and joiner Thomas Albinus Spofforth, the son of a herdsman from Castle Howard. He had submitted the planning applications for four houses in the street in 1894. Spofforth is listed as living in number 2 in 1898-9 directory. He worked on that and the house next door, as well as numbers 7-9, 15-21, 20-28. He also had plans approved for several of the houses in Queen Anne's Parade and elsewhere in the city. There is much joinery in these houses, fitted wall cupboards, deep moulded skirting boards, picture rails and turned spindles in the banister rails. Spofforth had planned to work on more of the houses but he died on 12 February 1899 aged 39. He left a widow and four children, including a baby son, Stanley Albinus. They are described as wards of Mrs Alice Anderson at number 19 in the 1901 census. At the next census in 1911, all but the oldest boy (another Thomas who would have been 22 by then) were living with their mother Eliza at number 28. She lived to be 71. There's a memorial window to her in St Olave's church.

An application for the completion of the last section of the street dated March 1898 is a fascinating document. It gives details of the owners of the already completed houses. At that point Spofforth owned the final plot on the even-numbered side of the road. I suspect his middle initial has been mis-transcribed as an R on these 1898 plans which show his ownership of many properties and plots. The final plot on the odd-numbered side is still owned by Jones.

In an agreement (with the deeds of Number 39) dated 27 February 1899, barely two weeks after Spofforth's death, Jones sells the land to the builder and joiner William Bramley for £600 to build 'no more than ten' remaining houses. Bramley pays a small deposit and will pay off a further £60 on the completion of each house. The neighbouring land it says belongs to 'the executors of T. A. Spofforth deceased'. The agreement says Bramley must not start building until the elevation and sectional plans have been approved by the vendor. He's to 'build the said dwelling houses in accordance with plans to be supplied and pay the vendor £10.10s for such plans.' Sadly no elevations or sectional plans have come to light.

The first title deed of my own house dated 1900, a handwritten, parchment document with lots of red sealing wax, tells me that Jones had earlier sold two plots of land on which my own and my immediate neighbours' houses now stand to this same builder, John William Bramley, for £120. The deeds also mention William Hepper, an architect with a brickyard in York, who had an interest in the property too for a short period. Was he involved in the design of the houses, I wonder? Or was Arthur Spottiswood Jones, an architect from Chelsea and the landowner's brother, one of the original mortgagees, a greater influence? There were agreements in the deeds about building the foundations (9") and the kerbs and the drains 'to the satisfaction of the urban sanitary inspector' for the whole street to Love Lane at the lower end. The road at the top end is marked as Mason Street on the plans.

There are very strict orders in the deeds of these houses that the owners 'will not let the properties be used as a shop or public house or ale house nor for the sale of intoxicating liquor nor as a means of exhibiting trade or advertising.'

The street first appears in the York's directory in 1896-7 with only nine residents listed. The even numbers which back onto St Peter's field progress more quickly; they are completed by the 1900 directory and the odds, which back onto Queen Anne's, by then reach as far as number 29 which is listed as vacant. At the 1901 census, the first to include North Parade, all the houses were occupied. The pattern of the buildings is clearly seen on the later map.

The houses have a half-timbered and harled gable which yokes together the larger of the front bedroom windows of neighbouring properties. This perhaps gives an impression that the houses are larger than they are. Only the width of one room and a narrow hallway, they are fairly deep. They all have the same curve to the downstairs front window. Tiny forecourted front gardens lead in through a small entrance porch. Some of the halls retain the original Edwardian tiles in terracotta, ochre and turquoise. Originally there were two downstairs reception rooms. The larger room faces the street, the back room, smaller by the width of the staircase, faces the courtyard; both had tiled fireplaces.

The kitchen, pantry and outhouses form the tapered leg of the L shape of the buildings, jutting into an enclosed courtyard. The kitchen would probably have had a cooking range. There is evidence of an original tiled hearth and a chimney goes up through what is now in many houses a spacious bathroom, but which would then have been the third bedroom and bathroom, a pattern which some houses still retain. Some still have a separate toilet upstairs. This area of the house situated above the kitchen is accessed from a half landing and an additional short flight of stairs. There would have been an outside toilet and possibly a shed for storing fuel.

Plots were sold off to different builders, so there would have been some variation in detail but all seem to originally have had a spacious front bedroom with two elegant tall windows which may have been divided into two sleeping areas by the early occupants. This and the second bedroom had fireplaces and wall closets. Some of the houses have grown upwards to lofts and outwards to conservatories or utility rooms or kitchen-diners or fourth bedrooms, reducing the courtyard area. Who, I wonder, first inhabited these spaces?

## Then and now: family life

*The move from multiple to single occupancy*

North Parade was a much more densely populated street in the first decade of the twentieth century than it is now. It housed predominantly the upper working/lower middle classes. Families were larger and some also accommodated relatives, boarders and servants.

In 1901 at number 37, for example, Henry Warrington, a 51-year-old railway guard, one of several residents employed by the North Eastern Railway, lived with his wife and seven children aged between 5 and 24 *and* they managed to find room for a single boarder, a joiner like Warrington's youngest son. Two older sons worked on the railways. Where did they all sleep? The neighbouring street in Queen Anne's was one storey higher. In North Parade there would have been no attic rooms then. It was common for the youngest children to sleep in the parents' bedroom. The older male siblings would have shared one bedroom and the girls the other. There can't have been much privacy for anyone, or much room for personal possessions. Nowadays it is common for even the baby to have a separate nursery and a lot of belongings to go in it. Perhaps the boarder rented one of the downstairs reception rooms? But this would be palatial compared to the conditions in Walmgate where families of this size could be sharing just one room.

Across the road from the Warringtons' at number 36 lived John Sunley, a gardener, with his wife and seven of their children aged between 10 and 26. The oldest of these, a daughter, was married but not in work. Her two older sisters had already left home! The three eldest sons were employed: an upholsterer, a railway fitter and a Government Ordnance Survey clerk. Ten years later in 1911 the couple, who came from a small village near Kirkbymoorside and who had been married forty-two years, would be enjoying a sense of space; only the youngest two children remained at home.

Not all the families were so large. In 1901 the Jeffersons who'd moved into the new house at number 29 had three children aged 6 to 12. Jefferson was an engine driver. His children grew up in the street. By 1911 the children are all clerks, the eldest, a girl, in insurance, the 19-year-old son is working for the railways and the youngest boy is clerk to a cocoa and chocolate manufacturer.

Their neighbours at number 39 were newlyweds in 1901. William Challenger (aged 24) was a commercial traveller for a coal and builder's merchants. Florence was only 18. By the next census in 1911 they have three children aged from 3 to 9. Families of three are rare now.

Several households in the street had boarders, mostly in their early twenties: an ironmonger (number 2), a bookkeeper in a news office (number 26), a millinery buyer (at number 28), a school teacher (number 34), a bookbinder (at number 35) a railway clerk (at number 40), a shirt cutter and an estate clerk (at number 15).

In addition to children and lodgers quite a few households had elderly relatives living with them. Thomas Monkhouse, a saddle-maker who has a wife and a young son seems to have been supporting both a 78-year-old widowed mother-in-law, and a 39-year-old sister-in-law who had no stated occupation.

There would have been no state pension when these houses were first built, nor care of the elderly, nor any unemployment benefit, though there was an Old Maids Hospital in Bootham and Ingrams hospital at the top of the road (built in 1630 and restored after the Civil war in 1650) provided almshouses for 'Ten Old Widows'. Carole Smith's fascinating study *The Almshouses of York* has just been published. There was still a workhouse at Huntington. The City had a Relieving Officer and Poor Law Guardians.

A handful of households are shown as having had 'servants' or 'domestics'. One of them, Ada Barnes, was only 14. She was in the home of Joe Hardy, a chemist's assistant. He and his wife had a 2-year-old son and a new baby. A couple of railway clerks had servants, as did the solicitor at number 22. All of these had a new baby in the family. In these smaller families there would have been a spare room for a servant, but it was common in Victorian England for the servants to sleep in the kitchen where they worked.

There were several servants' registries in York. Some correspondence in York City Archive dated 1915 about a female refuge called North Parade House led me at one point to believe this 'two year house' which trained female orphans and other 'wretched females' in laundry and domestic work was situated here. But the correspondence comes from Cheltenham where there was a North Parade House Refuge in Winchcombe Street. There is no named addressee and I can find no other evidence to establish such a refuge here.

There was no single occupancy of houses here in 1901, the nearest being an 87-year-old widow who had a young servant living with her at number 14. There were four other widows in the street named as heads of households who had children or other relatives living with them. All the other heads of household in the street were men. If they could have seen into the future as we can now glimpse into the past, I wonder what they would have thought of a woman living on her own in a three-bedroomed house?

Some of the original occupants had been married for four decades. None were divorced. The column on the 1901 census where residents record what jobs they do remains empty against the wives' names. By 1911 one has the temerity to explain she 'assists in the house'. It does give occupations for the older children. Warrington's 16-year-old daughter, for example, was a dressmaker. Today more than a quarter of the street is in single-person occupancy. Some of these residents have never married, one, in Warrington's former house, is about to move to share a new home with his civil partner who works in another town. Several are divorced. The vast majority of these single occupants today are women. Most have, or have had, a career.

## Then and now: origins
*Who first lived here? Where had they come from?*

At the time of the 1901 census the family living in my house had
come originally from Stourbridge, Worcestershire. Richard Rees
Tyrer was a 31-year-old lithographic artist. He had a wife Grace
and a 7-year-old daughter, another Grace, born in Eccles. I like
the sound of this family with its two Graces. I try to picture them.
I wonder if he worked for one of York's printers such as Ben
Johnson or the *Yorkshire Herald*, or perhaps he too worked for the
railway, designing posters, or railway timetables.

The Tyrers had another child, a son, in 1906 and were still here
in 1909 but by the time of the 1911 census they were living in
Derby. The head of the new family living in my house in 1911,
Squadron Sergeant Major George Potter, an instructor with the
Yorkshire Hussars, was born even further away, in Eastbourne. This
32-year-old had a 20-year-old wife, a 4-month-old son born in
York and his 15-year-old sister-in-law living with them. Further
down the street at the same census there was a civil engineer from
York whose wife was born in Scotland; the wife of the school
teacher at number 4 was born in India, but these are exceptions;
I can see they are not typical of other residents in coming such a
distance. It was much more usual for residents at that time to have
been born in Yorkshire, either York itself, or the outlying villages,
Haxby, Norton, Stillington, Lockton, or other Yorkshire market
towns such as Thirsk, Ripon, Bedale, Malton, Helmsley.

Henry Warrington, the railway guard at number 37, was
born in the tiny village of Saxton, near Towton, site of one of
the famous battles in the Wars of the Roses. He married a girl
from Ulleskelf 9 miles south of York. They were in York by

the time their last child was born in 1896. Warrington's move from Ulleskelf to York typifies the huge change from a national population that was 80% rural at the beginning of the nineteenth century to one that was 80% urban by its close.

I wonder if as a 16-year-old boy Henry had come into York to see the big Exhibition of Fine Art and Industry on Bootham Fields, the land in front of Bootham Asylum? The Exhibition, the first in the provinces, ran for three months from late July to the end of October 1866 and must have been a memorable experience. The specially constructed building which comprised a great hall, square pavilions and galleries was made entirely of timber and glass and lit by glass panels in a roof with a 50-foot span. The Exhibition was approached through new wrought iron entrance gates, bronzed and gilded. The highest attendance on any one day was 12,650 people. The success of this Exhibition led to a similar event on a much larger scale held at the newly built Exhibition Hall in 1879. More than half a million people attended. The building was sold to the Corporation in 1891 and became the City Art Gallery in what is still known as Exhibition Square.

I have interviewed only a handful of people living here today who were born in Yorkshire. Of these, Kath spent part of her working life in Australia. Teresa's son is currently stationed in Germany. Stan started his working life in the Cameroons. Janet and Stewart who have lived in Yorkshire all their lives have seen their son and grandchildren emigrate to Australia.

The residents now come from a much wider geographic area and more diverse cultural backgrounds. There are people here from the length and breadth of Britain. Of these, Ann, born in Southend, has spent part of her working life in Saudi Arabia; Kirsty, born in Cambridge, spent a substantial part of her childhood in Japan and her parents are currently in Singapore. Kildip's older siblings were born in the Punjab; Dorianne, born in Leicestershire, has a Belgian mother; Jo, born in Cornwall, has a

Polish mother and Ukrainian father. Patrick, whose father was in the army, was born in Germany, and spent some of his childhood in Malta. I have interviewed neighbours who have come to York from the Philippines, Hungary and Poland; neighbours who started life in Dublin and Bombay and a daughter of German refugees, born in India and raised in Bulawayo.

York is still perceived to be a very white city despite the notable presence of York's current Archbishop John Sentamu, the first African archbishop in the English Church. His wife Margaret, also Ugandan, has a role which encourages equality and diversity in the business world. The city's two universities have expanded their intake of overseas students. I was surprised, however, to see research published in February 2010 by the Joseph Rowntree Foundation which identified 92 different ethnic/national origins and 78 different first languages present in the city. (Mapping *Rapidly Changing Ethnic Populations: A Case Study of York*. Craig et al. <www.jrf.org.uk>.)

## Then and now: work

*What work did the first residents do?*

In 1901 the North Eastern Railway (which formed its headquarters in York in 1854) was by far the most significant employer of the street's residents. Wagon-building shops had moved from Queen Street to a larger site in Holgate in 1865 where a new carriage-building shop was opened in 1884. NER's huge office building went up between 1901-6.

The 1901 census records as living in this terrace: railway guards, carriage and wagon builders, a boiler maker, loco drivers and fitters, a railway signalman, a ticket examiner, a porter and fireman, several clerks and a cleaner for the NER. It is possible that some of the joiners and carpenters in the street worked for the railways too. Throughout the city of nearly 78,000 people – a substantial population increase in just ten years – the NER employed 5,500 men and boys. (Figures from *York A Survey 1959* pp. 120.) Census details have been included in the appendix.

There were several clerks and bookkeepers living in the street in 1901 working for solicitors, auctioneers, news offices, agricultural societies, ale porters and coal merchants. Coal used to be unloaded from barges on the Ouse at Marygate Quay for Hattees Coal Merchant which was just next to the old Bay Horse Inn. My neighbour John tells me his attic was four inches deep in soot when he first acquired his house. There were grocer's assistants and tobacconists, tailors and milliners, upholsterers and ironmongers, a printer's overseer, a gardener, a harness and saddle maker, a hairdresser, a traveller and just one person (at number 26) working as a cocoa and chocolate maker, York's other major industry at the time. There were one or two professional people

Bootham 1893 and 1909 before and after the building of North Parade.

# CAMBRIDGE HOUSE ESTATE.—BOOTHAM.
## — PRIVATE STREET WORKS. —

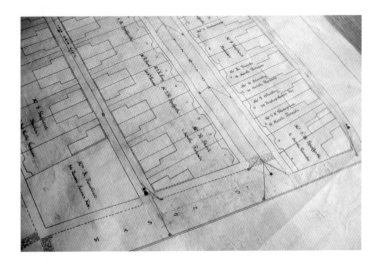

Cambridge House Estate. These 1898 plans show the owners of properties and remaining plots on North Parade and Queen Anne's Road.

Mr. J. E. Jones.

York Solicitor John Edmund Jones, landowner
and developer.

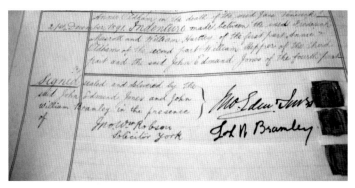

Jones' signature on deeds dated 1900 which refer to the earlier indentures
by which he aquired the land.

The Yorkshire Fine Art and Industrial Exhibition on Bootham Fields, 1866.

1905 entrance to the annual Gala held on the same site from 1858-1934.

1905 An alpine glassade owned by R Holdsworth at the Gala.

An organ grinder and his monkey on Bootham Terrace ca, 1900.

Crowds at Bootham Bar celebrating the Diamond Jubilee of Queen Victoria, 1897.

Looking through Bootham Bar from Petergate, 1905.

An Edwardian traffic jam – a carter turning into Bootham Crescent.

Coal barges are being unloaded on Marygate landing before 1895 – the old Bay Horse Inn is still on the right.

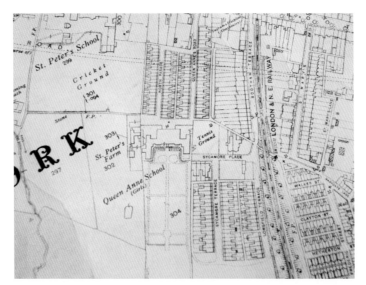

Bootham, 1929.

Extensive bomb damage to Queen Anne's Road. 29 April 1942.

and artists, a solicitor, an elementary school master, a painter of miniatures and a violinist who was also a professor of music.

It's clear that there were some young adults living at home with their parents who had no work, as well as others whose income would be contributing to the family. The only other evidence of unemployment I can find in this street in the census returns of a century ago is TB Wilson at number 25, a 58-year-old widower, 'formerly a master builder, now out of business'. But would people have taken boarders if they hadn't needed to supplement their income?

A recent BBC2 York-based documentary *A Life Without Work* (broadcast October 2010) recreated the life of John Addy, an unemployed man in York in 1900, trying to provide for his family of four. He was keeping diaries of his life, what he did with his day, what they ate (or more often didn't eat) for Seebohm Rowntree's groundbreaking study into the cause and effect of poverty. The research for this book, one of the most important written in the twentieth century, which influenced the creation of the welfare state, was done in Penn House, former home of the Rowntrees, on the corner of Bootham and St Mary's, which we pass on the way into town. The results were published in *Poverty, a Study of Town Life* in 1901. The BBC documentary was comparing the unemployment situation then and now and was deliberately timed to coincide with the government's spending review.

No one unemployed living in the street today came forward for interview for this book. But despite seeming a moderately affluent area of the city, there are people here who work hard to keep afloat. My interviews took place on the brink of a recession. A period of depressed interest rates had hit pensioners hard. Banks were collapsing and being bailed out. Financiers were still drawing huge annual bonuses. Libby's work in the Citizens Advice Bureau highlights the increase in individuals struggling with debt. Governments here and abroad were acknowledging huge national deficits. The first coalition government since the Second World

War brought in a spending review which threatened massive job cuts in the public sector in particular. Costs of food and fuel were rising. Benefits would be decreasing.

Work is still one of the major factors that bring people into York. The street has easy access to the city centre, the station and road networks for commuters. But the nature of the work has changed. The employer most often mentioned by today's residents is Aviva, the insurance company (formerly Norwich Union) which has its York Headquarters near Lendal Bridge built on Tanners Moat, the site of the original Rowntree's factory.

Today there is a much bigger service industry, with tourism playing a huge part in the city's economy. In the business directories at the turn of the previous century there were only six tea rooms or restaurants including the Railway Buffet and Betty's Café. Now there are thousands offering food from all around the world. Greg, Monika and Raf, Mario and Rami work in the hotel and catering sector. Katie and Michael and Jim work as actors and musicians. Fran is involved in York's annual food festival. Only a few have a connection with the older industries. Carol began her working life for British Rail; Will's first job in York connected, via Jarvis, to the railways. John worked for Rowntree's when he first arrived from Norwich, and one neighbour got his first graduate job here with their successor Nestlé.

Women's attitude to work has changed greatly over this period. Fran juggles three quite demanding part-time jobs, working mostly from home. Joyce, now 90 was reluctant as a young woman, despite being well qualified, to be in a job that expected her to use her own initiative. Karen, younger by four decades, was keen to set up her own business. The younger married women interviewed talk about the tension between the demands of a working life and motherhood.

The present backdrop is a society in which the gap between rich and poor has widened; two neighbours interviewed here were in jobs in which they hoped 'to make a difference' to this situation. It's a time when many private companies have closed their final pension schemes; when house repossessions are higher than ever before; when the young are increasingly struggling to get on the housing ladder; when the nation is debating how it can afford on the one hand to support its increasingly elderly population and on the other to provide university education for the young. Many of those now in work know they will have to work longer before they reach a pensionable age. Some, like Patrick, a physio, fear cuts in the workplace could cause increasing workloads. Stress at work is a significant factor today, as is the depressive effect of unemployment. I was moved by a timely re-showing of Alan Bleasdale's TV drama *Boys from the Blackstuff.*

Several of my neighbours have already reached retirement but have had interesting and challenging working lives. They continue to be actively contributing as volunteers and carers and many are still actively reading, learning, thinking; being creative in many ways. Those in work don't take it for granted and are constantly dealing with change. Some are lucky in that their work is, as Peter explains 'more than a job – a way of life'. Greg refers to his hotel as 'his baby'; Monika works long hours as a housekeeper but still takes a pride in what she does. For others, like Raf, their main interests lie beyond the workplace. The young are still aspirational, studying an increasing number of subjects as well as becoming fluent with new technologies. But they're facing a huge rise in university fees and a world in which one on five youngsters are unemployed. The lucky ones will find work that not only helps put a roof over their heads, but gives some job satisfaction too.

## Then and now: housing – ownership and tenancy
*Movement and stability; first homes and last homes*

In her book *The Victorian House* (2003) Judith Flanders suggests that in Victorian times only 10 per cent of families were home owners. It was quite common for families to agree short leases of three or seven years at most because they moved frequently as their circumstances changed.

The Tyrers, resident in my house in 1901, do not appear on the deeds so would have been tenants. In 1902 this and the neighbouring property passed from JW Bramley, the builder, to Betsy Halder, married to a furniture dealer, and Hannah Bruce, wife of an antiques dealer in Stonegate, for £560. It looks as if my house was an investment property. The purchases are made from the women's separate monies, a situation enabled by the Married Women's Property Act of 1893.

The builder Spofforth bought the property at number 1 in June 1895 for £500 and sold it on to Ralph Ness, a railway clerk, for £690 in the autumn of the same year. I was surprised a railway clerk could afford the mortgage but thought perhaps rent from his lodger helped to offset that. But I was more astonished when I was able to access the 1898 plans, where all plots are ascribed to owners, to see that Ness had initially owned not only number 1 but numbers 3, 5 and 13 as well.

Although neither the Tyrer nor the Ness family were still resident here in 1911 there was continuity of occupancy in ten of the houses between 1901 and 1911. There were still eleven people in the street employed by NER. Two sisters Hester and Mary Garton, who were living with their widowed mother in 1901, still both single and both dressmakers, are by 1911 heads of the household. Their young boarder is a weaver. Similarly Mary Dixon who lived with her widowed mother at number 15 is head of a boarding house next door by 1911.

Home ownership, which peaked at 70% in 2000, began to drop slightly last year. Whereas it was once possible to offer as a deposit 5% or 10% of the house price some societies are now looking for 25% of a much higher average price. The credit crunch has made mortgages harder to acquire causing frustration for would-be home owners. The Council of Mortgage Lenders states that the average first-time deposit is [in spring 2010] £34,000 – for many equivalent to much more than a full year's salary. This is nearly triple the average deposit of three years ago. Unsurprisingly 80% of first-time buyers receive help from their parents in getting their first deposit.

Some residents in the street today are simply renting a room in a shared house. For others like Michael and Katie, the house here is their first rented home after living in flats or bedsits. For Kirsty and Simon it is the first home they have owned. For several it has seen the start of a marriage, a relationship or a family. For many like me their home here has signalled a return to independent living at the end of a marriage. For others it represents a need to 'downsize' either on the death of a partner or parent, as in Vera's case, or with the prospect of retirement as in Dorianne and John's story.

A handful of the people interviewed have been in the street for more than three decades, several for two decades or more. Some were recent arrivals, others on the point of leaving when I talked to them.

Just a few of the houses here are investment properties to provide income through rents and as a better way to see capital growth at a time of low interest rates. Both Jim and Greg became landlords having acquired their houses from a parent. There are others (not interviewed) who began living in houses here, then retained ownership and rented them out when their jobs moved them abroad. A couple of solicitors currently working in Dubai rent their home out, another neighbour made a move from Nestlé in York to Kellogg's in Lancashire and then was posted to Canada for a few years and from there to Australia where he now has a young family.

The tenants interviewed here are Will, Michael and Katie, Raf, Monika and Istvan; Mille and Rosalie and their families were outgoing tenants of the property where Dan and Libby now live with their young son.

Will and Trish moved out of their rented accommodation soon after their marriage. The house they own now has only half the space of the house they rented. They are struggling to squeeze in the things collected over recent years.

I bought my house in 1995 for just under £70,000. Prices here have nearly quadrupled since then. I could not now afford to buy my own house. I am one of very many women in my age group who are rich in capital because of house price rises yet low on income because of time spent caring for family either out of work or in part-time working. As the breadwinner of my family at the point we separated, I had to ensure that both my husband and I could have mortgage-free accommodation. They would have been smaller houses without a timely bequest from an aunt. I don't know how people manage on a small pension, without additional income, if they have rent or a mortgage to pay.

I am aware that there are couples in this street who are not so fortunate, who are trapped in one home because of the housing market when they feel they need to be living separate lives. There may be elderly women living here surviving on only the state pension and I am aware of other residents who supplement their income and add interest to their lives by taking in 'York Associates' for bed, breakfast and an evening meal. These are European or Scandinavian business people who are on short courses at one of York's language schools; so the street has very interesting temporary residents too.

## Leisure in the Edwardian Era

Some of the first residents of this street may well have taken their young families to the Children's Fête which was held on Bootham Fields to celebrate Queen Victoria's Diamond Jubilee on 22 June 1897 or they may have joined the crowds at Bootham Bar on the same day? I guess children living here would have been amongst the 15,000 who attended Coronation celebrations for Edward VII on Bootham Field in 1902.

An annual Gala was held from 1858 until 1934 on the same field in front of what was known then as Bootham Lunatic Asylum (now Bootham Park Hospital). This is one of John Carr's many elegant Georgian buildings. (Others include the nearby Bootham School.) The Gala drew a lot of visitors with its produce displays and the fair. Perhaps some of the children here would have enjoyed the Alpine Glassade, the helter-skelter of its day, or had a chance of a hot air balloon ride?

Did the children see the organ grinder and his monkey pictured here in Bootham Terrace in 1901? Perhaps some families would have taken the train to Scarborough for a day out together, or have gone to York's purpose-built swimming bath at the bottom of Marygate (clearly visible on the 1929 map). Open-air with public access, this was owned by the Yorkshire Philosophical Society who had laid out the Museum Gardens and owned the Observatory there.

Perhaps families took a walk round the city walls? They could access the walls at Bootham. Steps were added there in 1889. Its Scandinavian name hints at a very early settlement here. They were lucky that Bootham Bar, the northern gateway to the city, was there at all. Its barbican was removed in 1831 and the

31

whole gateway would have been removed too, but citizens raised objections at a public meeting in 1832. The Corporation paid £100 for the repairs and the remaining £200 was raised by public subscription. The inner front was completely rebuilt: the arrow slits are a mistaken piece of 'restoration'.

Across the river the Railway Institute had been built on the site of the Railway Tavern in 1889. The railway workers from our street maybe called in on the way home to use the library, read journals or went back later to have a game of cards or billiards with their colleagues. It is now home to a multitude of clubs and sports organisations. Or perhaps they headed for the Bay Horse Inn on Marygate, rebuilt in its present position in 1896 to replace an inn of the same name which had stood on the other side of the street. (The Bay Horse has recently reopened after extensive refurbishment.)

In February 1902 the Theatre Royal reopened after a major refurbishment, its interior decorated in white gold and emerald green, to compete with the newly opened Opera House. The better-off residents might have splashed out for a special gala performance on 16 July 1904 when Sarah Bernhardt appeared for one night only in La Dame Aux Camélias. Ten shillings and sixpence for the dress circle. Two shillings even for the gallery. Local people remember special feast days on Clifton Green each May Day and pageants in the Museum Gardens by Tempest Anderson Hall. (See Van Wilson's *York Voices*.)

The river which at that time still had an active commercial role now sees regular sculling races, and the plying up and down of Redboats and tourist cruises out to the Bishop's Palace. Narrow boats such as *Tranquility* and *It's Enough* are moored here alongside small cruisers, the *Alter Ego* and *Lady Sophia*. This tree-lined riverside walk into town, now renamed Judy Dench Walk, comes to life with the annual Viking festival and charity fairs. The Sticklebacks River Café, providing teas, lunches, ices, is regularly moored here in summer.

Many of the buildings we pass today and the parks we walk though in our daily routines will be the same as those experienced by the first residents of the street. They would not have known that their lives were about to be changed by the First World War.

## Where have all the children gone?

In 1901 there were more than fifty children in this street aged from 0 to 16. In addition there were many older children living at home well into their twenties. The families were large despite the high infant mortality rate at this time. In 1900/01 deaths of children under 5 in York accounted for 42% of the total number of deaths of all ages that year. 30% of those were under 1 year old.

There was an understanding at that period of links between poverty, poor sanitation and child mortality rates. In 1901 statistics for infant mortality in Bootham were 169 deaths per 1000 births compared with Walmgate, one of the city's poorest areas, where there were 254 deaths per 1000 births.

I was reminded of the high infant mortality rates of the period watching the BBC2 documentary about the life of John Addy, who came from Hungate, an equally poor area of York. It was made clear that the 4 children this unemployed man was trying to feed in 1900 were the only survivors from 22 births. I'm aware that my maternal grandmother had a child every other year for 25 years. I began to wonder about the gaps in ages in the lists of children in these houses at that time. The 1911 census collects information from mothers of total births: a separate column for the number who survived to that point and one for the number of those who have already died. It tells me that the Warringtons, who by then had moved out to Moss Street, had lost 3 of 9 children. The schoolteacher's wife in North Parade had 6 surviving children from 8 births.

In September 1895 the Medical Officer was talking about the densely packed middens in the narrow yards behind some of the city's houses: 'Considering how many of these middens are daily receiving infected discharges from typhoid patients, the danger from such polluted air must be a factor in the cause of the epidemic... The ashpits and other filth receptacles, which are always full when the removal depends on private enterprise, would prove powerful agents in spreading the disease in the event of cholera breaking out in the City.'

The MO asked the sanitary committee, 'to seriously consider the advisability of extending the already improved water-carriage system. This would involve the total abolition of all midden privvies and the universal adoption of small dry ash receptacles and waste closets or waste-water closets.' He was asking for 'a bye-law to allow them to disprove any building plan which does not provide adoption of the water-carriage system.'

In the same bound book of minutes appears an advertisement *For Adams and Co Water Closet Manufacturers on Peasholm Green.* Perhaps our houses had proper plumbing from the start. There was certainly a toilet in the outhouse in the yard.

In 1901 smallpox, scarlet fever and typhoid were prevalent but there were also many accidents. The MO considered, 'there is much carelessness and ignorance as to the rearing of infants and much want of cleanliness... improper feeding... dangerous foodstuffs.' He produced and circulated a huge list of instructions about childrearing, hygiene and feeding which included many sensible things, but also the dictum, 'Never give a child fruit!' There is still controversy today about regimes of feeding and weaning infants.

It was heartening to see a copy of Joseph Rowntree's speech on receiving the Freedom of the City in 1911 commenting on the improvements in health, housing and education in the city since his own boyhood. By then the death rate had reduced to 11.9 per thousand and the school leaving age was raised to 14.

The street in its early days would have been full of the sounds of children playing tag, bowling hoops, doing hopscotch, skipping, chanting rhymes. It would be another three years before the first car was registered in York.

The school at the bottom of our road was the highly successful Queen Anne's Grammar School for girls. The first residents here would have seen this built. South facing with gables and tiles in a William and Mary style it was designed by one of York's best-known architects, WH Brierly, and opened in January 1910. It rehoused pupils from Brook Street Pupil Teacher Centre and was originally known as the Municipal Secondary School for Girls. Only when a second such school opened at Mill Mount did Queen Anne's take its new name from the street it was in. Children would have arrived on foot or bicycle and goods by horse-drawn carriage. It continued as a grammar school until 1985 when the city's education system was reorganised. When I first came here it was a comprehensive school but falling rolls led to its closure. The property was to be sold. Quite an anxious moment for the street's residents – would there be a new development there?

The bid accepted was from the nearby St Peter's. They wanted the building for a preparatory day and boarding school for 8 to 13 year olds. It was renamed St Olave's. Most residents welcomed the fact that the site remained a school, albeit one which, despite reassurances to the contrary, generated increased traffic. It houses a day nursery too.

Not only are there fewer young families here today but the families are considerably smaller. One of my former immediate neighbours, a primary teacher, found it financially and physically tough trying to organise childcare for two girls and return to work when they were small. She and her family moved back to her parents' farm when her girls were toddlers. They would gain more space to play and a Gran to help.

There are perhaps four or five households with young families at the moment. As none had come forward for the book initially, I phoned two former neighbours, Francesca and Kildip, who explained their decisions to move when their children were still very young.

I was pleased to be contacted later by Dan and Libby and glad to be able to include their story. Their son, born here in the summer, was enjoying his first Christmas.

Many young families today tend to move out of the terrace to more spacious accommodation when the second child arrives. They seem particularly to aspire to more garden space and are also concerned about school catchment areas and league tables.

Carol is the only woman interviewed here who not only originates from York and went to school here, but has also brought up three children, now in their twenties, in this street. Carol's eldest daughter, Becky, tells me that she and her siblings and friends played out happily in the street as youngsters and there was easier access to the school playing field at the bottom of the street.

The children we see now are mostly strapped into the back of their parents' vehicles being ferried to and from school. But it's good to see some of the street's residents walking past with prams and buggies, perhaps heading, as Carol did when hers were young, for the river or the Museum Gardens or the Holmstead play park.

# Sketches of Neighbours' Lives

## Elizabeth
*Changing worlds*

The novelist Kate Atkinson, an old girl of Queen Anne's School, came to fame with her first novel set in these streets of York, *Behind the Scenes at the Museum*. In it women from three generations of a York family have moments of epiphany when they realise, in a blinding flash, they have been living the wrong life. There was such a moment in my own life which led to my move to this street.

My son and daughter were already in their late teens, early twenties enjoying life at city universities by the time I moved here. I was moving out of the family home where they'd grown up, on the edge of Thirsk, the market town where I started my teaching career, where I met their father, a physics teacher at the same school, a rural comprehensive; I loved the school, the work and the location.

There was a romance, a marriage, a miscarriage, and a year later I must still have been very much in love to have agreed to swap the gamekeeper's cottage where our married life began for a top-floor flat on Grosvenor Terrace with a view across the railway line to the grounds of Bootham Park Hospital. Mark had arranged a sabbatical for himself to do a degree in York and told the Head I would be leaving! I knew nothing of the history of Bootham Fields then. It was 1971, a precursor to the 'Winter of Discontent'. There were strikes and electricity cuts. By the time I'd established myself in another school it was time to move back to Thirsk where Mark still had his job. We bought a house way beyond the street lights, not my first choice, though a good place for a family, with space for sandpits and chickens and bikes.

Some men do extreme sports. Mark did extreme DIY. The week before our son James was born I woke to see autumn mists swirl in through the back bedroom window, and swirl out of the front. The windows had not been left open; they'd been removed altogether – so much easier to do a thorough job of the decorating if you took the whole frame out! It was November. When Kate was a toddler the staircase disappeared. Out it went; banisters, treads, risers, the lot. In came a ladder for six months.

After twenty years of DIY I woke up to the fact that everything we owned in this house was turning tobacco coloured. Mark, such a sociable man when we met, had retired into a world of TV and home brew. While he had built the house and I'd rebuilt my career, the marriage had foundered. To survive I needed a different world.

There was heart-searching and house-hunting, there was hobbling on crutches after a fall on black ice; there were disrupted plans, broken chains, and the kindness of friends who gave me temporary shelter before I finally moved into North Parade in January 1995. From first sight I felt this house with its book-lined lounge and leafy courtyard was meant for me.

I had exchanged a home where sheep by far outnumbered human inhabitants for a quiet but central city location and a very peopled street; the views of the Hambleton Hills for Bootham roofscapes and the amenities of a city; a marriage for 'single occupancy' – an independent life, but one rich in friendships.

Years of short-term contracts teaching Literature at Ripon and York St John (York St John University now) which had been such a lifeline in my wilderness years, had developed into a permanent lectureship. It seemed a privilege to be sharing texts which opened young minds to totally different worlds. It was a job which constantly provided new challenges and opportunities. A Teaching Fellowship gave me chance to design web-based learning resources to introduce the study of poetry and women's writing. Bigger than books in one way, these for a while were my new babies.

My work provided me with many strong friendships too. Living here I was a short walk from the York campus and an easy commute to Ripon where initially my office was based, and where one of my closest colleagues, a writer, still lived. For many years we managed to retain a special bond of friendship that centred on many shared interests in writing and art, even though we were living in different cities. He provided me with a home from home. Another friend from work and his wife who gave me a lot of support in my move to the city also provided me with a welcome in their second home in France.

I've always had a good network of women friends. Two of the closest from that period, Jane in Thirsk, a social worker who was responsible for my involvement in local politics and Community Care, and Isobel, a colleague who lived up on the moors and became a walking companion after I returned to part-time work in the new millennium, died far too young and are still missed.

Getting into rural North Yorkshire was still very important to me – but I chose to live near the centre of the city. Having theatres and concert venues and cinema within easy walking distance when I surfaced from teaching and writing was just such a treat. Having good friends and neighbours with whom to share these experiences has been even more important.

The development of City Screen cinema complex in the former Yorkshire Herald building seemed to open up the city. I caught up on film-going after two decades of abstinence. I was also given the chance to bring scores of fascinating writers there including Alan Plater, Jackie Kay and Simon Armitage who made their experiences so vivid. The final speaker I introduced on campus, Imtiaz Dharker, a highly respected poet, artist and film-maker born in Pakistan, described how disturbing it was after 9/11, the defining moment of the decade, to see herself in the eyes of others mutating into a terrorist; at the airport for example, when her passport was given a much longer than usual scrutiny.

Kings Manor was just a short walk away. A friend encouraged

me to be a student again. I joined a class there – *Drawing for Non-Artists* – and this became the start of an absorbing new interest. I looked at the world differently from then on.

Having my own space to think, read, write, paint and relax with friends and family has been really important to me. In my own time I began a book about my favourite poet U.A. Fanthorpe which took nine years' gestation before it saw the light of day! At the heart of her work was the importance of people. They are important to me too.

My children both lived here briefly, James for a year or so when he was struggling through a patch of low-paid jobs before his Open University degree gave his career a new direction; Kate for a short while just after she'd graduated. Now across the Pennines she juggles a full-time job as a textile technologist with the demands of motherhood. Now I juggle my retirement projects with grannying, the best job of all! In 2009 my twin granddaughters inspired a little book of poems for their fifth birthday.

Their visits have let me rediscover York with fresh eyes. It's been great fun introducing them to the theatre and riverside walks. Museum Gardens has become *The Squirrel Park*; they love the newly refurbished child-friendly Yorkshire Museum, where you can play with mosaics, or design new bugs and assess their chances of survival. Ingrams Hospital has become *The House of the Eleven Dwarves*. (Only the central doorways with their borrowed Norman Arch would accommodate a grown person.) It has been good to have the house filled with laughter.

My own childhood was spent in a very different street. Coal lorries thundered down the road at the front of my house to Bentley Colliery, where my father was Head of the Finance Office. He'd moved from Eastwood where he'd started work as a clerk at 13 at the private Barber and Walker Mine. He'd qualified as an accountant through correspondence courses. It was VE day when they moved – my brother remembers the bonfires. I had given little thought to the ten-year gap between myself and

Harry, till a teacher in our first week at grammar school asked us all about older siblings. 'So you're an afterthought?' she said. I was baffled when the class erupted in laughter.

I arrived in the big floods of 1947 soon after the nationalisation of the mines and the birth of the National Health Service. The house and a generous supply of coal came with Dad's job. It was to be my home for seventeen years. Not a magical childhood, though I loved the transformations that may blossom brought to the woodland at the back where we had dens and the way snow turned the ugly slagheaps into toboggan runs. My mother, the youngest of twelve children of a Durham miner, taught drama. She deplored the eleven plus, which branded her pupils failures and built their confidence through acting. Her school pantomimes brought some magic too, as did the world of books.

Summers in my early childhood meant Whitby. Before Dad had a car (round about the Coronation when we bought our first television too) we went in Old Reynolds' taxi. The top of the big trunk was filled with produce from the garden for the landlady. They'd keep saying, 'the sea is just over the next hill' and suddenly there it was, the best magic of all.

Not yet 7, my granddaughters are already seasoned air travellers. Despite living in a world of celebrity culture, addiction to the *X Factor* and *Strictly Come Dancing*, they still enjoy the simple pleasures of conversation, story and pantomime, sea and sand. They love Whitby too.

'Next door' was an important place in my childhood. The engineer's wife and daughter became a surrogate gran and auntie to me. It felt like an extended family, a close neighbourliness not repeated till my friendship with Jill in this street. Though the pithead winding gear, the landmark that dominated my childhood, is long since gone – Bentley Colliery closed in 1993, less than ten years after the miners' strike, and the area is now transformed into Bentley Community Woodland walk – I still remember my fascination as a child with the way the two halves of our coal-board semi mirrored each other in layout, but inside revealed two totally different worlds.

Now I have a similar fascination with forty-three terraced properties which on the outside are almost cloned but on the inside reveal very different worlds.

By the time I came to write these sketches of neighbours' lives some were already my friends; others were acquaintances or neighbours I knew by name; others I had never met before the interview.

## Peter
*Murder and madness – music and motorbikes*

I must have moved here the same time as you – I was wanting to buy the house you got, but wasn't prepared to raise my bid. So I'm curious to see it again. I like all these original features. I'd been living in Holgate for about three years in a house of a similar vintage. I was commuting to Teeside Poly at the time; I worked there for about ten years, but when I got home I didn't feel as if I was in York, it was too far out. I wanted to move to the centre.

I first fell in love with York and North Yorkshire when I was working down in London and living with my then wife and son in Hertfordshire. It sounds ridiculous, but we saw it as a hidden gem, almost an undiscovered place. When I first moved York's Barbican Centre had just opened. [*It was short lived. Built in 1989 this leisure centre, a major venue, closed in 2004. There are plans to reopen it without the pool.*] It seemed to signify progress for York. There were still people who lived and worked in the city. It still had a soul. Now many of those jobs have gone. It's much more a tourist centre. I've loved being nearer the centre of things, but I feel the street has lost some of that community feeling that was there when I first moved in.

The demographic changes in the street interest me. It would have been built for the upper working class – some of the houses go back to the mid 1890s. They weren't all built together. Then it got gentrified. Then 'studentified' if that's a word – student ghettos are certainly getting nearer. We've seen the increase of multiple-occupancy with more 'buy-to-lets'; I very nearly rented my own house out soon after I moved here. I'd got the chance of a job in New Zealand – it was all tied up with a relationship but both things fell through.

I've been at Leeds University for fourteen years now, but would hate to live in Leeds. Though I did once toy with the idea of getting a flat there. I was in a relationship with someone from Bristol; we would have had our main house there. But no, that didn't happen.

*Peter's work is quite unusual. I confess that I had 'Googled' him and found this terrifying list of publications about murder and madness. He laughs.*

Well, my background is in medical sociology. I've written and taught a lot about the sociology of health and illness. I gradually got into forensic psychiatry and it's taken off, partly because it's popular with the students and the media. But it's a double-edged thing. It's given me a living, but it's a horrible area to be in. I cringe sometimes when I hear myself speaking about it. And I can't stand the glee on the students' faces when I outline the course. As part of my research I have been invited to observe investigative processes and I know what it does to the officers involved and the secondary victims of these murders.

I can't bear violence in films. It's sickening to think of it being turned into entertainment. With the exception of Morse, I can't stand detective things on TV either. I'm about to do some research into the huge popularity of those things, the psychology and sociology of the nation's addiction to violence. The gender bias of crime fiction interests me. Anyway I don't have a TV though I do sometimes see things on iPlayer. I like *In the Thick of It*. Cutting-edge satire.

I miss Borders bookshop. [*Borders closed at the end of 2009.*] I used to do a lot of my writing in there in the Starbucks café on the first floor. I'm trying to find another urban office. Tried out Café Nero today, but they kept trying to sell me pastries when I only wanted coffee.

Finding time for research, given other workload pressures, is becoming ludicrous. In fact I've just delivered a conference paper… a bit of a diatribe. It might get me sacked. But I'm too belligerent to care. We're in the hands of the managers and bureaucrats. I don't know how we've allowed it to happen, to be reduced to this world of 'outcomes' and business-speak. I'm not careerist. I've never chased after the next step up. It's my way of keeping some control over my life, not getting overwhelmed with work. I get to work at eight in the morning but I'm out of there by four come what may. Consequently I still enjoy most of what I do, though I'm completely out of favour. Leeds University has to make huge savings, but they've had their fingers rapped for making pre-emptive moves on redundancies. An awful lot of jobs will go. There's a strike this week. What I do is not a job; it's a way of life: losing that would be awful.

I do have a life beyond work. I play saxophone and I'm in a couple of choirs in the city; in fact we're performing in the Theatre Royal soon, which is a bit scary. I do the gym; I go dancing once a week; I swim – in fact I used to swim at York St John's baths before they were built over. I just went in, said to the guy in charge, 'Leeds University owns this and I work for them so I should be allowed to swim here too.' And he let me. Great!

You'll have noticed I've still got my North-East accent. I was brought up in early childhood in Newcastle, but schooled in Gateshead. Dad was a medic; my mum, who died recently, was a seamstress; she became a factory worker. My dad cleared off when I was about four, although I did develop a good relationship with him later, and we were plunged into poverty. So because of that experience I'm torn between that middle-class ethic of progress through education and a kind of fatalistic disrespect for it.

I think my world outlook was also influenced by the time I spent with ex-hippies. I did quite a bit of travelling between school and my sociology degree in London. I was drawn to a sense of warmth, of spirituality about these people; but conventional religion's not important to me. I'd subscribe to Richard Dawkins' views.

I've had my house on the market recently. Took it off, partly because of the building work next door; and I couldn't show people round when I've an Australian family coming to stay soon. I've got a bit of a love-hate relationship with the street. I campaigned vigorously against the traffic generated by the school here. That still winds me up. I'm a street rep now.

My real problem is the motorbike. I've had motorbikes nearly all my life. The current one is a Moto Guzzi Classic 750. I might get a Breva next. But there's no garage here. It's almost impossible to get it in and out of the yard. That's the main reason I would move. But there is a fear of change. Acknowledging that annoys me. I have good neighbours at both sides though. They're very understanding about the saxophone. We've negotiated when I can play. As they've pointed out, 'if you move, you could do a lot worse.'

*Interview 23/02/10*

## Kildip
*A juggling act – recruitment, work and motherhood*

I came to York because I was engaged to Daniel, a York man, who had a job with the Press Association at Howden. We'd met in Leicester, my home town, when he was working there as a journalist. My two older siblings had been born in India in the Punjab. It would be the mid-sixties when my parents came over here and I was the first of three further children. Dad had come over first; he already had a brother in Leicester and got a job with Dunlop. Mum and the family joined him two years later by which time he had a home for them. She had work in a foundry called CORA which was quite well known in its day.

I desperately needed work when I came to York so I went to a recruitment agency in Davygate. They asked what I wanted to do and I said I'd try anything. I explained that my background was in sales/marketing/admin and that I liked working for people. I thought, *I could do what they were doing.* They liked the sound of me and said, yes, they would like me to work for them rather than sending me out temping, so that's what I did. I loved it. My role was to visit existing clients and also to find new work opportunities for people. I would call in to explain to businesses and organisations the value of using temps to cover for sickness and maternity leave and give some literature. I kept an eye out for new work places. I loved meeting people and was quite successful in finding openings for workers.

*My son, James, remembers Kildip calling at Tower House when he was working for a security firm there, remembers not the recruitment literature, but how beautiful she was.*

We first saw the house in 1997, but it was under offer then.

51

Then it came back on the market in 1998. I remember the agent referring to this street as 'The Mayfair of York'! But the house was a mess; it had been owned by York University and had housed students in separate units with fire doors, so we got it for a very good price. We married in the August, renovated the property, put in nice fireplaces and so on and really felt established in the street. So by the time our first child Alex was born in January 2001, we had a group of surrogate aunties and would-be-grans eager to babysit which was wonderful! Teresa and Ann and Dorianne and Sue who all lived at our end of the street were really helpful – they seemed to compete for turns at the job! And we adored Stan and Rummana, our next-door neighbours.

*When I pass on this compliment to Rummana on our way to the theatre that evening she remembers her surprise and delight in discovering she had an Indian neighbour in what was then a very white city. Kildip, she remembers, used to bring home a whole caseload of Indian food freshly cooked by her mother after her trips back to Leicester!*

I went back to work supposedly for a three-day week when Alex was six months old, possibly too soon, and found this a really hard time. No one had been keeping on top of the sales and marketing so there was a lot to do. Alex went to a nursery two days a week and had one day with his gran. But I was riddled with guilt; I felt he was all over the place. It would sometimes be 5.30 or 6 before I could pick him up. It was especially hard if he was teething or had a minor infection and was grizzly. And there was more work than could be done in three days. So that only lasted three months.

I handed in my notice and then: What a relief! I allowed myself to enjoy a much happier routine that involved lots of shared activities with my child: *Babyswims* once a week; *Songbox* mornings in a hall where a lady got the youngsters to enjoy percussion instruments and singing; and a creative session at the Steiner school each week. Lovely! Jasmine was born in 2003 so all my time was taken with the children then. It wasn't until Alex started school in 2005 and Jasmine went to a nursery, Joseph's at Rawcliffe – I feel really confident with the care they provide – that I started back working two days a week.

By now I was with a Finance House – a business that helps people find mortgages, pensions, loans. I was doing some admin for them, but you know what it's like when you're a part-timer – it inevitably spreads to more hours than I wanted to work. I'd find myself dealing with work things on my mobile in the early mornings and late in the evening. So that ended too. Now I'm just doing one day a week admin for a trademark attorney. I also work as a teacher's assistant at the children's school, Park Grove, and I'm doing a course on working in schools.

Daniel's hours are fairly regular, but I've always been the one to do the school drop-offs and pick-ups. He's no longer in journalism. Situations change and you have to adjust. The part of the firm he worked for was bought out by Orange and France Telecom. So now his work, which is predominantly product promotion and management, involves a daily commute to Leeds.

We moved a short distance out to this larger house off Clifton Green when Jasmine was just two weeks old. Not ideal timing, I have to say – two major life events so close together! We simply needed more outside room for them to play and grow in. Here we have a long back garden and plenty of space for toys inside. But that first house in the North Parade was the happiest house we have ever lived in – there was lots of social activity. I remember meeting neighbours at the street barbecues and going to people's houses at Christmas, and the Millennium meal. And do you remember that Diwali party I did? But Daniel and I have discussed this and we've already decided – when the children are grown we will downsize and relocate to this lovely street!

*Interview 22/10/10*

## Francesca
*In love with English Heritage*

We first came up to York in 1991 and immediately fell in love with the city. Trevor, my partner, was in London working for English Heritage but had an opportunity to move to York. We didn't want to go back to an impersonal city. With his Heritage background Trevor knew this terrace was unique in York in its architectural coherence. A pretty street – we loved the pleasing Edwardian design – most of the original windows seemed to have been preserved, and the interiors had lovely detail: cornices, deep skirting boards, old fireplaces.

Trevor knocked on the door of the house opposite and asked to see the loft conversion. If we were to have a family we might need more space. That's how we met Sue and she's been a friend ever since. We were married from here in 1992 at the Registry Office in Bootham. Sue came to the wedding. We all walked down to the Ouse from there for a riverboat trip. The reception was in the Merchant Adventurers' Hall where we danced in the Undercroft.

I suppose the fabric of the house mattered given Trevor's job, but it was also a street with a sense of community which centred on Stan and Rummana. We really valued them as neighbours. They had a party at their house every Christmas, without which we wouldn't have met other neighbours. Jo and Carol across the road were always friendly and we met other young families in the street. Kildip was a very bubbly neighbour. She raved about our dark green living room and followed suit.

We loved being so near the centre of York. We used to walk once a week to Tempest Anderson Hall in the Museum Gardens to the Film Society and would often meet up with Stan and Rummana there. It was great having Whiting's Deli at the top of the road. I remember Mrs Whiting left a bouquet of flowers on our doorstep when our first child, a son, Finbar, was stillborn in 1995.

I'd been working for the Open University in Manchester before I moved here. I loved working for them and had hoped to transfer, but there were no vacancies in this area. I found part-time work teaching Literature at York University initially and did some Continuing Education courses. From 1993 till Eppie was born in 1997 I worked full time at Scarborough College. We didn't do the extension in the end and moved to have more space. Phoebe must have been conceived here the night before we moved out to Ouse Lea. [*An award-winning Housing Association complex with landscaped communal gardens on the northern outskirts of York overlooking Homestead Park.*]

*Phone interview December 2010*

*I remember visiting an art exhibition Francesca had curated in her home at Ouse Lea. The family moved from there to Harrogate. Francesca, one of the first women to graduate from Balliol College Oxford, did research into the letters of eighteenth-century Bluestocking Mary Delany. More recently, as a lecturer at York St John University, she had been working with creative writers and artists on a Tanka project that involved collaboration with the Yorkshire Sculpture Park and Japan.*

*Francesca's family, friends and colleagues were shocked by her untimely death in April 2011. She was buried in York cemetery surrounded by birdsong and cherry blossom following a humanist service there. Francesca was 51.*

# Sue

*Down on the allotment – medicine, art and artichokes*

*Sue, a petite, energetic cyclist, with an infectious laugh, was one of the first people to befriend me when I came to live here. Will she have time to be interviewed? Saturday's no good, she's going to a Jazz festival; Sunday afternoon she's planning to go to a VW fair at Northallerton. Perhaps she was about to fulfil a recent dream and buy a camper van.*

*(P.S. She did, but conscious of her carbon footprint, she now car-shares with a neighbour!)* 'Would I like to join her at the allotment on Sunday morning?' *I would.*

This isn't about how much good food I can produce. It's about the experience of being in the open air, having some exercise, enjoying all this, *she says with a laugh, broadly gesturing at the open views on the Rawcliffe Allotments off Shipton Road.* It's also about enjoying the life, the subculture: each patch is individual, like the street; there's time for banter with the other idiosyncratic characters who rent these plots and make them their own.

*Sue is passionate about food, about healthy eating.* I've left *The Food Programme* recording. Last week's episode was about the Slow Food Movement. *Sue has been travelling down to the University of Surrey every three months for several years to study Nutritional Medicine. It's taken a lot of commitment; involved the 'painful' writing of 54 essays.* I can't see myself doing the long dissertation for an MSc.

*Sue came to live in this street in 1992 at a point where her marriage had broken down.*

I'd been with my partner for ten years, been married for the last seven of those. I suspect my job didn't help. I was a salaried partner in a General Practice in Leeds then. Perhaps I wasn't a good listener, or, perhaps I'd done my listening at work. I changed tack in my career and became a School Medical Officer; I did General Practice one morning a week and also a family planning clinic. That was quite tough when there was no sign of a family for us. My background was in microbiology and pathology. I'd done paediatrics in Oxford, casualty in Warwick, and GP training in Edgware before coming to York.

My current specialism is in GU (genito-urinary) medicine which is a conversation stopper! *She laughs.* I'm not really keen to talk about it. It is a sensitive area of medicine. I deal with the more familiar problems of skin infections, herpes, warts and gonorrhoea; I sometimes see patients who are HIV positive and refer them on to specialist colleagues. As for the much-publicised rise in chlamydia I think some of this is simply that more people now are willing to come forward to seek diagnosis and treatment; less stigma is attached to the clinics. And, with the rising divorce rate, we are not just treating youngsters.

*She admits shyly to an academic interest in probiotics and genital flora.*

I'm resistant to being defined in terms of my career. As a youngster I toyed with the idea of being an architect but perhaps my father's unfulfilled ambitions of being a doctor were transferred to me. Trained as an accountant, he had a textiles factory in Macclesfield where I grew up. There was this particular old mill he rented which I loved – something to do with the way the light filtered through it, its smell. Dad was in with the golf club crowd. He sent us all to boarding school in Wales; it was the done thing. On balance I would have been happier *not* to have gone away to school.

I'm the eldest of three girls. There had been a boy who had died in infancy. My middle sister, a rural environmental scientist, has recently emigrated to Tasmania with her husband and three children after the Foot and Mouth outbreak put an end to their business. I'm hoping to go out quite soon to visit. I'm closer to my younger sister. She lives in Derbyshire with her family; her son was born after IVF treatment. I see them quite often.

Our mother's schooling had been interrupted by illness. She'd met my father when she was in the WRNS and he was a Royal Navy Volunteer. She had secretarial skills but did no paid work after she was married. It wasn't a happy marriage. Mum, encouraged, I suspect, by the new evangelical vicar, used the church as an escape from problems at home. The first year of my own marriage was a difficult time for me. It was the year both my parents died.

*Though a medical practitioner by profession, Sue is an artisan by temperament. She is an accomplished painter; friends are treated to delightful watercolour miniature cards at Christmas; a loom dominates the front room of a house which she likes to keep simple – almost minimal; there are sea-grass floor coverings and painted walls which show off a few original paintings, prints, and woven wall hangings, many of them the work of friends. They're hung from the picture rails on old fashioned curvy brass picture hooks. The dining room is full of objects which recall specific people or places: a collection of shells, bladderwrack and small pieces of driftwood gathered on a ceramic owl plate by York artist Mark Hearld; a terracotta mask,* 'done by an artist friend who lodged here'; *a piano stool that was once her husband's.* 'Things still get swapped back and forth.' *An oak carved chest she's storing for a more recent friend. An elegant but simple polished wooden chair that was her father's. Books piled on the shelves on medicine, mushrooms, monasteries, monoprinting.* Nothing has happened to the loom as yet, *she laughs*, but I have plans.

*Sue has a deep-seated interest in a whole range of hand crafts.*

No. Don't say textiles; that's too pretentious. Just say I like fiddling with things. No don't list all these strands – it sounds too scatty.

*I realise the word 'hobby' simply will not do. From her words and the way her hands try to sculpt a delicate shape in the air, I realise that our deepest aspirations are fragile and that to attempt to name these things that matter, things that are fluid and somewhat elusive, leaves her feeling vulnerable. And I suddenly realise how hard it will be for me too to put it into words, to post that letter through doors – to say, 'I have this idea that's been in my head for years to tell the stories of the people in the street.' To make it happen.*

Do come to our York Artworkers event next week; a textile artist, Sue Lawty, will be talking about her projects. It's hard to explain how she works – she does these subtle things with rock, raffia, linen and lead, including vast wall hangings for the Victoria and Albert. You'd like it.

I do go. Tempest Anderson Hall is full. It is inspirational. I decide to join the Association, of which Sue's been a member for some time. She pursues her wide-ranging interest in art through gallery visits, workshops and field studies and experiments with different media. The last course, Painting Pollinators, brought together her interests in natural history and painting.

*There are a few pollinators about here in the early autumn, attracted to vivid patches of cosmea and nasturtiums dotted amongst the bean rows, onion beds and ornamental grasses. Sue is fighting a hopeless battle against Mare's Tail. The plot which belongs to a friend Clare is now shared three ways with herself and Janette. I lend a hand by thinning out the raspberry canes and am sent away with a pocketful of Jerusalem artichokes to throw in my next casserole. I could take to this!*

*Autumn 2008 and 16/02/2010*

*Sue introduced me to many of the street's established residents, including Stan and Rummana with whom she shares a keen interest in art, and Kath who organised several street parties.*

# Rummana

*Bombay, Kobe, Paris, London.*
*Vibrant paintings and a colourful life*

*Rummana – a colourful name?* 'Yes, it means one segment of a pomegranate and is equated with a ruby.' *And Rummana has led a colourful life, 'shambolic' she suggests. Her house is full of colour: rich wallpaper with exotic birds; Indian wall hangings in deep rose, purples and golds, brought here from her frequent visits home. Her tiny courtyard garden in York feels exotic with jasmine, camellias, bamboos, a little fountain, decorative birds.*

*It was at one of Rummana's house parties that I first met many of my neighbours, and over the years I have got to know her well. She was born in Bombay, an artist and editor. I'd been privileged to see a catalogue of one of her early exhibitions of vibrant oil paintings; stunning. Imagine my embarrassment when, enthused by some work I'd done on an art course in Ullapool, she insisted,* 'You will show me how you do these acrylics. I will come to your house and bring sandwiches and you will teach me. This is something I must do.' *We had fun, but oils are more sympathetic to her favourite landscapes.*

*Rummana makes annual trips home to her beloved Kihim. This beach in India south of Mumbai is the 'magical place' of her childhood. A few years ago it suffered tornado damage. She grieved for the many lost trees. The following year the trip home with her granddaughter was delayed after the shocking news of the Mumbai massacre (27/11/08). Coordinated gun and grenade attacks by fundamentalists were targeted at British and American tourists in luxury hotels and restaurants but also killed and injured many Indians.*

*She explains how Kihim was acquired by an ancestor 150 years ago when his friend, the British rep in Mumbai, was auctioning off land.*

5 km of beach for a song. He sold it off in parcels so now all our extended family have a beach hut there and spend our winters together. My daughter Naella and her three children visit and keep in touch with their Indian family this way. Any door they knock on is a cousin or an aunt and they get their mangoes. It is one of the most heavenly places.

*Rummana's next comment takes me totally by surprise:*

My earliest memory, however, is not of India but Japan. I would have been about two – a vague image of a leafy walk. It was Kobe. My father and his brothers owned a cotton business – they took turns to do three-year stints out there. I had an *amah*, a Japanese lady who was devoted to me, the youngest of her three charges. Another early memory back in India is of the evening gatherings of poetry recitals and music. As a child I would sit entranced.

It was when my mother was in Japan that she began to write; so many people asked questions, they wanted to know about this intelligent, outgoing lady in the beautiful saris; so she began a memoir about her childhood in Hyderabad, which later turned into a novel. Some of the happiest times of my childhood were spent visiting our grandparents there. They had a long bungalow with extensive gardens – you could hold bazaars and ride horses there. It was magical. All my cousins would congregate. I've recently rediscovered my middle cousin. I had two days in Delhi with her last year thinking back to this wonderful time, how we plucked fruits fresh from the trees, the perfume of them. The servants were like family; they had been there forever. Hyderabad was a beautiful city then. Awful what's happened to it; land is at such a premium. Now it's an IT city like Mumbai with ugly high rise buildings. The beautiful public buildings have survived, but they are dwarfed. There were of course no planes then. The visit from Bombay involved an overnight train which was all part of the adventure. I remember each time we set out father would present me with a brand new sketch book and colour pencils. I was expected to fill this over the holiday. I'd been encouraged to paint and draw from an early age.

We lived in Bandra, a suburb of Bombay subsequently inhabited by film stars. My mother, not only a writer but an astute business-woman, bought up a lot of land when we were young at a time when you could buy vast pieces of land for very little. My first school was a local Catholic Girls' School. But at ten I went to the English Cathedral High School in the city centre. It involved a cycle ride, a walk, a bus and a train journey and another walk! Hard to believe that was our daily routine. All our further education was financed by Mother selling off a piece of land as each of us reached that age. I learned from people who came to speak to me after her funeral that she'd also paid for the education and medical bills of a lot of poor children in the area.

In 1948, the year after Independence, the family had a bumper year for business and Mother who had long wanted to travel took her chance. My sister and I went off to boarding schools in Lausanne and Montreux while our parents toured Europe. I learned French, learned to ski. I loved that year (my sister hated it), but returned to Bombay to finish school. My older brother went to Birmingham University; he made friends with the son of a Serbian family who'd fled from Yugoslavia and made their home in London. They invited us to visit and we spent a whole year in the UK. They became a second family to us; even now they are our sisters and brothers. My sister stayed on at art school in London. I followed quite a broad curriculum at Bombay University then did art school. I had the opportunity of one-to-one lessons with two impoverished young tutors, who later became leading Indian artists – Ara and Husain.

My mother's book *Zohra* had just been translated into French so I went with her to Paris in 1956 for the launch. It was so exciting. I stayed on for three years – started at the Ecole des Beaux Arts, but found the approach too traditional; I became bored. I'd already done that, drawn a hundred statues. Soon I had the chance to move on to a private Atelier de L'Art Sacré – *much more interesting* – twenty of us – no heating, no food, no coffee, just SPACE and some very good teachers. I learned about new media: stained glass, painting, ceramics. I had a small exhibition with a Polish friend in a Polish Literary Club. Then despair; the three years was up; I didn't want to go home.

I had met an Indian journalist when travelling to Paris, the only two Indians on the plane. Our paths crossed later in Delhi and, in the face of huge opposition from my parents, we married and lived for a while in the north of India. As a result of several successful solo shows I was invited out by the Australian government to an arts festival in Adelaide. We spent a whole month out there. My daughter was born in 1962, but the marriage failed as my parents had predicted, so I divorced and went back to live with them.

I ran an art class for children in an orphanage and taught in Bombay in the mid-sixties. It was there I met Stan, in a swimming pool I remember! We married in 1969 and here we still are. The new marriage was good, but this was not an easy time for me. Stan's term of work was over; I was teaching in a Montessori school, trying to keep on with my painting, and had my daughter to think about. So Naella went to boarding school in the north for a year while we sorted out jobs and a home in England.

*Rummana tells me about her work as Information Officer at the Tate Gallery.* Marvellous! I loved it there. I stayed for thirteen years and made lots of friends. We had some wonderful parties at our Hammersmith riverside flat. Ideal for seeing the boat race. Many of them will be coming to York next month to help me celebrate my 75th birthday. Of course at that time, with a house to run, no longer a battery of servants, and a challenging new job, I had no time to paint.

I had acquired three step-children and Stan's youngest, Sally, lived with us for a while and my daughter got to know her well before her year out travelling round India. Not long after that Sally was killed. *Devastating* for us all; Stan will tell you about it.

Some years later, Naella was back from the States with a degree from Columbia University working for JP Morgan in London, where she met her husband. Then another bleak time; there was a car accident – Naella was badly hurt, had to delay a family. We went to and fro to visit. By then we had retired early and were living in York. We were made welcome from the start; a neighbour knocked on our door saying, 'I will introduce you to Julia who knows everyone.'

Now, I'm lucky my family have moved to York and are living round the corner. Naella's career has moved into counselling; she's currently working on a project helping parents and teachers understand teenagers, which must help with her own brood too. So I see a lot of my three beautiful grandchildren. The eldest, Catriona, seems to have a lot of creative energy. She writes poems and paints. She has just had a work experience week at the Tate. The middle child, Alexander, has recently had a term in an Indian school. This was his idea; he wanted to learn the language. It was wonderful to meet him there last year. The youngest, Samuel, is a chorister. He knew from very early on he wanted to sing. He says it's a good day when he wakes up and knows he will be singing. We love to hear him in the Minster. The Advent service is especially magical. But he's just at the age when his voice is likely to break. You must go and hear him.

In retirement I've been busy writing. A close friend from Cambridge asked me to edit an autobiography of a French mediaeval poet, Christine de Pisan, the first European professional woman writer. Fascinating, but a huge task. I had to research all the historical background and piece together a life for her. It took five years. I was immensely proud of it. Compared to that, doing my mother's book was a doddle. I'd promised her before she died that *Zohra* would get the editorial attention the first edition lacked. I had to hone it down and knit the story together. I kept the original preface by E.M. Forster, of course. It was a good day when the new edition appeared.

And now I realise it must be thirty years since I have done any serious painting. Hearing you talk about your classes I feel a real need to get back to that.

*Interview 27/04/10*

## Stan

*A banana boat to the Cameroons,*
*pharmaceuticals in India and the finance of fine art.*

We've been here twenty-two years. We moved to York in July 1988 when I took early retirement from Bonhams – one of the big three arts auction houses. I was Finance Director and Company Secretary. I'd told them at interview I had an Indian wife and she was rung up. She was Head of the Information desk at the Tate Gallery at the time. We felt they were checking her out, needed to hear her voice; they were all terribly refined there. No Estuary English allowed. A very cultured world. They all had *mummies and daddies in the country* you know. [*Stan mimics a mouth full of plums.*] My office opened onto the auction rooms so when I was having a break from my number-crunching I could wander round the galleries, look at the jewellery, the porcelain and fine art. It was a good atmosphere. I've enjoyed all three of my careers, but by the end I had become mentally and physically exhausted by the relentlessness of deadlines, deadlines, deadlines. You simply couldn't miss a deadline. Monthly accounts, unremitting budgets, filing company returns, distributing minutes, dealing with lawyers. It was definitely time to go while we still had health to enjoy it.

We had no responsibilities, grown up children, and a lot of equity in our London flat, so we decided we would live elsewhere – leave behind the buzz of London for somewhere quieter and less expensive; we made ourselves a little laundry list, and York ticked all the boxes. We could easily keep in touch with our London friends here. It was sheer luck getting this house and it has been one hundred per cent the correct decision for us.

My first career was in the Colonial Service in West Africa.

*I can imagine Stan running things in the colonies. For all his years he still has an authoritative voice, a sense of decisiveness and presence.*

I'd grown up in Leeds, apart from a brief spell at Upper Poppleton as a child evacuee on the outbreak of war in 1939. I'd been to Roundhay Grammar School, studied geography and economic history at Leeds University and one month after being demobbed from National Service in 1954 set out on a banana boat for the Cameroons. I'd been offered a short service commission in the army but I had known for a while what I wanted to do; I had this job in the Colonial Service lined up and I didn't want to delay. The country had been carved up into French and British Cameroons by the League of Nations after the W.W.I. Peace Treaty. I worked in the Ministry of Finance. A lovely, peaceful place to live, although, *he laughs*, we were all issued with *The Green Book – Health Hints for Officers* with graphic warnings about problems from malaria to dysentery and the dreaded unpronounceable onchocerciasis (nicknamed onkyponk!) that gave you blindness. You worked for eighteen months then had eighteen weeks leave plus two weeks' travel time each way for a return home. Wonderful!

The next posting was Sierra Leone. My family were with me there. My first wife didn't work. Like all colonial wives she went to coffee mornings. My son, the eldest of three children, had been born in Leeds but our two daughters were born in Freetown. Sierra Leone was granted Independence in 1961 and we were asked to stay on till the African government was embedded. But it was a lost cause; a few years on we were asked to leave. We sold them the Westminster model of administration. Awful to see it collapse later through corruption and dictatorship. It makes me *sick* to think what has happened in that lovely place – the chaos, the diamond smuggling, the civil war, the problems with their neighbouring countries.

I came back to England early in 1964 without a job. Luckily I still have a Colonial Service pension and we got 'Harry

Lumpers' – a cash compensation for loss of office. It was a chance encounter with a friend who worked for Guinness that led to my next job. At that time Guinness had just acquired an old trading company, a conglomerate that traded all over the old colonial empire. They needed someone to standardise the system of accounting, reporting and inspection for the companies involved. Would I be interested? Yes I was. I went out to India for a preliminary visit in 1965 and discovered the managing director had his hands in the till. I had that job for seven years. So I was overseeing a complex mix of companies including Smith and Nephew, largely involved in manufacturing of surgical products and pharmaceuticals. We built a new factory in Bangalore to manufacture local anaesthetics for doctors and dentists; we were making toothpaste, surgical sutures, all sorts of new products were developed. The government needed us to develop as prior to that Johnson and Johnson had a monopoly. They didn't like that. The firm went from strength to strength; shares were floated publicly in Bombay.

It was while I was in India that I met Rummana and her 6-year-old daughter Naella. We were married in India in 1969, a second marriage for both of us. We moved to London in 1974 when Rummana found her job at the Tate, and it was there by chance I saw the advert for the job at Bonhams. We'd established our home at Barnes in London in this wonderful flat overlooking the river at Hammersmith Bridge. Mind you, Barnes was a no go area then. You wouldn't get a taxi driver to bring you over the bridge. My youngest daughter Sally had become great friends with Naella. Then this most awful day; a knock on the door and the police telling me Sally had been murdered. She was in her third year doing a biology degree at Brighton. She'd set out to the airport to meet her boyfriend on his return from a holiday, and we never saw her again. Apparently she'd gone home with him to Dulwich, where he'd slit her throat.

*I flinch at the brutality of the act and the unflinching delivery of the comment. How do you come to terms with such knowledge, such a loss? I have other friends who've lost children, a cot death, a childhood cancer, a road accident, a teenager bullied into suicide, a young woman claimed by pneumonia, all unbearable. A violent death must be particularly hard to come to terms with. I think of Peter's comments about the secondary victims of violent crime.*

He'd gone to a police station and confessed. We'd no idea there was any problem; he'd seemed an ordinary middle-class boy; but there were obviously mental health problems. He was locked up in Broadmoor or Rampton, I forget which. She would have been 21 that year. A long time ago. This year one of my grandchildren will be getting married. He's 24. Something good to celebrate.

I still think the Nineties was the golden age for the street; we saw a lot of our neighbours, Francesca and Trevor, Daniel and Kildip, and we were very friendly with Julia – Jill's predecessor. And of course the Padré; Geoff and his wife have moved out to a bungalow now. Joyce was a real character. And we saw a lot more of Kath in those days.

## Kath

*Retired gynae ward sister; the £10 scheme to Australia*

*As I wait at Kath's door, I'm shocked to realise there's graffiti on the wall next to me. I'd seen 'street art' in the underpass under the Scarborough railway line on our route into town, but wasn't prepared for this. She reassures me it was just a solitary incident.*

I'm a bit exposed here on the end but it's better since they put the security cameras in at St Olave's School. And I've got the advantage at the end here of the extra space. We've had some good barbecues here, haven't we. Time we did it again. There's quite a few new people now.

*Kath seems to know everyone.*

I have lived here more than thirty years, you know, but I didn't start here. I was a country girl – brought up on a farm at Bolton village 12 miles away. That's another reason I like being at the end here, being able to see trees. Trees are not always a good thing, though. Do you remember, when that one came crashing through the gable wall and chimney pot? Nearly midnight it was, one Christmas Eve. Not what I was wanting Santa to bring!

*Kath ushers me in:* I used to apologise for the chaos, now I'm older I don't bother. Come on in by the fire.

*We go into the back room – it's very cosy and homely with some nice pieces of mahogany furniture; some started their life in the farmhouse, others she's treated herself to recently. I've never seen such a large electric fire and every bar is blazing. There are books and papers and photos about. Kath clears a chair for me.*

You'll see my motto on the mantel: *an immaculate house is the sign of an unlived life.* That's Lola curled on the hearth rug. She seems to have adopted me – she really belongs to Lisa down the road.

*The sleek Siamese doesn't stir but a much larger, hairier cat comes to investigate. Perhaps I've sat on his chair.* Don't worry about Felix, he's just nosy. *Kath is one of a network of cat and dog owners in the street who help each other out to cover for holidays.*

As a girl I travelled in daily to school at St Margaret's in Micklegate. My mum had became very ill when I was about 10; she'd had a stroke. I was just 17 in 1958 when I applied to be a nursing cadet. Full nurse training started at 18. I spent time in the County Hospital and Deighton Grove, a convalescent home then. In second year we could live out. I shared a flat round the corner here in Queen Anne's Road for three years. That's when I first got to know this area. That was a great time. In fact last year we had a big 50th reunion. Do you know, we met at eleven and didn't get home till five! I think they wanted us out of the restaurant but there was a lot of catching up to do!

Then I qualified to be a staff nurse and worked at Fulford in maternity, gynae and theatre. Such a lot of lifting involved! And not the equipment they have now. My first month's pay was £7! I lived out at Fulford for a while.

I came to live in Bootham again in 1967. I had an attic over the paper shop – it was a chemist then. My dad worried 'cos there was no fire escape. Cross's, the fish shop, was there before it moved to Clifton – I nursed Mrs Cross. Now they just have the market stall. There was a fruiterer where the launderette is now. They were bowlers. The local bowling club closed last year. Whiting's Deli was there even then. I'd been at school with Mrs Whiting's daughter Pat, so she kept an eye out for me.

Anyway, I'd always wanted to travel and in 1968 I got this chance to go out to Australia. We'd done Australia and New Zealand at school and I had cousins out there so I knew a bit about it. There was this £10 scheme! Accommodation was free in the nurses' home and there were better salaries by comparison to Britain; but you didn't go into nursing for the money. At first I worked in theatre at the Royal Women's Hospital attached to Melbourne University; then in casualty in Toowoomba, Queensland. I thoroughly enjoyed it. Mind you I've never been a beach person, but I loved Australia. Melbourne was like a small English city, Brisbane more like a market town. It was a sociable time. I cooked meals for lots of friends.

When I came home in 1972 I returned to work at Fulford; I saw this advert and I thought 'right I'm going to go for it' and I got the post of Sister on gynae. By then my pay had gone up to £55 net per month. I remained a ward sister till I retired. After the Salmon Report (1966) you were responsible not only for the care and safety of patients, but organising your team and teaching students on the ward. You were seeing people at a very special point in their lives; there was some heartache, a few harrowing tales, but mostly you saw a lot of happiness, a lot of happiness.

Then Fulford hospital closed as did the County, City and Military hospital. A new District Hospital replaced them. Ridiculous, squashing it in on Wigginton Road where there was no room for expansion. It should have been built on the Fulford site, you know, where the Designer Outlet is now but apparently it was 'too far out'. Here you are, you can borrow this book about it that Chris Dowell wrote. You'll find some of me in there.

*In the group photos Kath is the short one at the front. There are some anecdotes in this and she tells me some more, not for the book, involving airing cupboards and baths.*

I was living in a flat in Bootham Terrace. I still had friends round here. A friend told me: 'You should really think of buying.' I spotted a For Sale sign in this street at number 28. I really liked it, but I dithered; I wasn't sure I'd be able to afford it and was beaten to it. When this corner one came on the market I made enquiries. I discovered a mortgage would cost less than my rent! You've never seen anything like it. What a state! I remember a kitchen unit disintegrating when I touched it. I think the phrase is, 'Has Potential!' That was February 1979. I moved in April. I'm still doing it up.

A year after I moved the flood waters came within an inch of the grating. Then in 1982 just out there the snicket was flooded and I saw a boat sailing past the end of it. I busied myself making tea for the police and the army. I decided it was the only time I'd be likely to be carried over the threshold.

No, I never married, though I'm not just an old spinster, you know. My sister married the boy next door and he bought the farm my parents had worked as tenant farmers. It came up for sale just when my dad was ready to retire, when I was in Australia. So there she is with three children and quite well off. But I've *done* things. We're in touch but don't see a lot of each other. Our lives went different ways.

Come into the kitchen while I put the kettle on. It's all just been refurbished – I'm really pleased with the layout. Do you like the duck egg blue?

*I do like it and the William Morris willow pattern paper. It's very pretty. But I'm puzzled by the most enormous bag of potatoes by the sink.*

I've seventeen friends coming later this week. I shall make a comfort meal and they can chip in something for the Angels charity [*for children with leukaemia*]. Do you remember the Millennium progressive meal? We had starters in one house, mains in the middle and puddings at the end.

*Kath still loves her food, but tells me she's been advised to lose weight. She's getting a bit breathless these days.*

When I retired I took a friend's advice, and got involved. I joined the local History Society. Do you know Nevil Shute once lived at the top of the street? I'm off with Friends of the Art Gallery to Glasgow next month. I like to get out and be doing something. I don't really like sitting in the house. Tim's a lovely neighbour. I often go across and have a natter with him, don't know what I'd do without him. I volunteer at the Treasurer's House each week and go once a fortnight to Nunnington for the National Trust – I'm a life member. The local branch organises group holidays too. I'm on the project committee; run fund-raising events. William Hague came. You'd have enjoyed that. He talked about *Walking in the Dales*.

*I leave Kath to tackle her mass catering. She opens the inner door with a lovely stained glass panel she'd designed.* 'With apologies to McIntosh,' *she adds, as she looks out.*

I often wish I had a metal detector; there must be treasure in these snickets that pass the end of the street – when you think of the people who've trod this way over the centuries. And you know about the bomb don't you, that fell in the school fields in the Second World War? They were aiming for the station and some bombs overshot. It did a lot of damage to houses round here. They found shells in the fields and Clifton Ings.

We must have another street celebration when the stories are collected.

*Interview 16/02/10*

*It was at Kath's street barbecues that I first met many neighbours, Kildip and Daniel, Jo and Carol, John, Vera, Ann and Teresa.*

Stan and Rummana

Kath

Joyce

Jo

Carol

Ann, Sue and Jo at Joyce's party.

Francesca

Sue

Kildip, Daniel, Alex and Jasmine

Teresa

Vera

Kirsty and Simon

Janet

Peter

John

Ann

Tony and Pat Hugill. Last Day of trading at Whiting's delicatessen 31/03/10.

# Whitings Deli

*Shutting shop*

*We didn't know it at the time of my interview with Kath but Whiting's Deli was about to close. Kath and I were both there to wish them well on their last day of business at the end of March 2010. In the counter, now empty of food, they had spread a display of archive photographs of Doris's prize-winning cheese counter and window displays.*

---

**WHITINGS OF YORK**

NOTICE TO OUR CUSTOMERS AND FRIENDS

THIS IS TO INFORM YOU THAT PAT AND I WILL BE RETIRING AT OUR YEAR END ON MARCH 31 2010 AND AS A CONSEQUENCE THIS SHOP WILL CLOSE ON THAT DAY.

THIS EVENT WILL BRING TO A CLOSE AN ERA OF FAMILY SHOPPING AT WHITINGS.

IT HAS BEEN OUR PRIVILEGE AND PLEASURE AND BEFORE US THAT OF NORMAN AND DORIS TO SERVE GENERATIONS OF CUTOMERS AND TO CEMENT MUTUAL RESPECT AND FRIENDSHIP.

ESTABLISHED IN 1951 IN THE DAYS OF POST-WAR RATIONS THE SHOP MOVED TO THESE PREMISES IN 1959.

AFTER BEING AT THE HELM FOR NEARLY 60 OF THESE YEARS WE ARE LOOKING FORWARD TO OUR RETIREMENT AND WOULD LIKE TO THANK OUR CUSTOMERS FOR THE SUPPORT THEY HAVE GIVEN OVER THE YEARS AND HOPE LIKE US THEY WILL REMEMBER THE SHOP WITH AFFECTION.

TONY AND PAT HUGILL.

---

# Jo

*Wars, weddings and ping-pong*

*Jo is a wedding photographer. When my daughter Kate was married at the Treasurer's House in 2002 it was Jo who captured images of that special day for us.*

That would make a good photograph!

*Jo is looking at a bike being gradually assimilated into the ivy at the end of my jungle of a yard. It's my son's, I tell him. He's supposed to do the last stage of his commute from Ripon on that to keep fit!*

Well it needs rescuing. I've got this thing about bikes; if I hear one squeaking I have to get my oil can out. I am a born-again cyclist – it was table tennis got me fit in the first instance. I'd been very fat as a youngster; I started playing at a church youth club and have played ever since. In fact, *he laughs*, here's a sign of a misspent life – I'm a record holder! I played more table tennis for York in league games than anyone else, as a junior, an intermediate and a vet!

*Jo is such a lean, fit guy it's hard imagine a fat version.*

I was bullied and teased about it. Games lessons were pure torture. But I was fat for a reason. My mother who was born in Vilnius survived the Russian invasion of Poland. She'd been taken to work in Russia, and moved on through Persia, where my older brother Andrew was born, then to Kenya and South Africa. I'm not sure of the exact itinerary; she doesn't talk about it much and I don't like to ask to stir up painful memories; but we've found her name on the passenger list of the *Winchester Castle* which left Africa on 15 August 1945 for England. My mother eventually reached a resettlement camp in St Mawgan in Cornwall where I was born. But I know she'd lost everything at home. She was from

76

peasant stock – had a small-holding. She picked up Russian. She didn't want me to resemble the starving children from those years of hardship, so I was fed *vast* plates of food. I saw it as a challenge to eat as much as I could.

There was no dad about, but a lovely uncle who I really bonded with. I only saw him sporadically but we got on so well when he visited. There were several further moves. My first clear recollection is of the toughness of starting school in the Cotswolds, of not being able to speak a word of English. Another reason to be picked on. I remember a camp there at Springhill – lots of Nissan huts – lots of Polish families. I'd be 7 or 8 before we moved to the outskirts of York at Sutton on the Forest.

I'd been told my dad had died at the battle of Monte Cassino. It was only when I was about 12 that I found out, in a rather brutal way, this was not the case. I wanted to join the Air Training Corps and had to take my birth certificate. It said, 'Father Unknown'. How could that be? I knew who my father was. Then a mate at school pointed out to me that Monte Cassino happened in 1944, four years before I was born. It took a while to work out that it was Andrew's father who had died in that battle. My father was in fact the lovely 'uncle'. He'd been in the Polish army, escaped from the Russians only to be captured by the Germans and ended up in St Mawgan where he'd met Mum. They hadn't been able to marry because the war had separated him from his first family. He already had a wife and sons in the Ukraine. I'd seen photos of them. My half-brothers I realised now. Why hadn't they told me before? That really affected me badly. I felt there was a stigma somehow. We never really talked about it. I was really fond of my dad – gutted when he went back to the Ukraine. I was in my early twenties. I can still remember that trip to the station wishing I could somehow stop him going. I knew I'd never see him again.

I missed the eleven plus because I had appendicitis. It's always rankled that I didn't get a second chance. I ended up in Burnholme Secondary in York. I left after GCE's. I felt I needed to start earning money to support my mum, so I got an apprenticeship at Vickers Instruments, initially in optical engineering but fairly soon moved into the photochemical side of things. I did detailed work under microscopes; then I'd produce graphical images of this stuff for the arms trade. We all had to sign the Official Secrets Act. I realise now all that close work did for my eyesight. It was a ridiculously unsafe environment, working with poisons and asbestos-lined fume cupboards – we accepted it as the norm then. I suppose that's what led me into photography; there was a darkroom there and I was printing up things for friends.

I was doing well. I'd married a lovely lass from work when I was just 22. We had our own house, but after a year or so I felt too settled somehow. It might have been different if there had been children. I was restless for new experiences. I decided to branch out on my own. It wasn't easy to start with. I worked with a printer called Mac from a garage with a window on Bishopthorpe Road. Great fun – but no money in it. Then I worked for Saville's photo shop. I set up a studio there and ran York's first ever baby photograph competition. Then I thought I could make it on my own. I found a shop in Walmgate, but had to work shifts at Rowntrees to help pay the rent. That's when I became a Kit Kat addict!

After Vicky and I split I seemed to fall on my feet. I found the perfect studio in St Mary's; things looked up. I devoted myself to photography. I had as much work as I could handle. I was getting a good reputation and making a good living. That was when I met Carol; she was working as manager at Elliott's Hotel round the corner. Quite a tempestuous beginning! I got jealous of another guy she was seeing. I broke in and confronted them – cut myself on the glass and had to be taken to the hospital to have it seen to. *What was all that about?* she wanted to know – so I proposed the following day. This was a second marriage for her too. Carol had been a footballer's wife – York City not England. We stayed in the basement flat at St Mary's then moved here before Becky was born.

In the early days things were going well. Carol was finally doing the nursing she'd wanted to do – Kath was involved in her training. But then two big changes happened. The property where I had my studio in St Mary's was up for sale. I couldn't afford to buy the whole building. I'd found an ideal alternative and was just about to take out a second mortgage for a studio in Exhibition Square when the shock announcement came that a third child was on the way. This was Jan. He's great. He's a really good referee – one of the best in the North – but at the time in the face of this news, I decided to abandon the idea of a studio and work from home. I can see now it must have been difficult for the family, especially at Christmas. The whole house would be colonised by photographs. Sometimes it would be Christmas Eve before it was all sorted. Just magic; suddenly the tree up and the candles. I loved that.

I suppose I started doing more of the domestic things and less photography while Carol advanced her career. She's a practice nurse out in the country. Loves it. Perhaps inevitably, life took her in different directions emotionally too, and so the break-up began. Things are tough at the moment. The only people benefitting are the solicitors. It feels surreal, as if I'm in some sort of limbo. I'm glad I've got good neighbours.

*Because Jo works from home he seems to have become an unofficial neighbourhood watch for his end of the street. Jo keeps keys, silences burglar alarms, waters plants, ferries the sick to hospital appointments, hunts for lost cats.*

I've been a wedding photographer for thirty years now, but this last decade the world's moved on into the digital age and people are doing more of their own photos and reprints and videos. I'm still passionate about film photography. There's such a plethora of photographers now, I worry about the profession becoming deskilled. As soon as the domestic situation is sorted, I'm hoping to have a 'relaunch'!

The two girls are in their twenties now. Becky had a bit of a wild time – went off to Scotland with a girlfriend – but she's back now. She joined an art therapy group – thought the tutor was great. Their work is on display at City Screen. Helen's OK now. She has a flat in Acomb, but it's so hard for youngsters trying to break out of low-paid jobs. On the way up there's a point where they lose that bit of housing benefit – they really need a minimum of £200 a week to make it worthwhile.

My mother's still going strong at 93. I cycle across to Acomb most lunchtimes ostensibly to feed her – but she's still feeding me! I do an hour's circular tour, and on a *very* rare occasion if I think I've earned it I stop for a pint at the Tollerton Boot and Shoe – a real bargain at £1.40 a pint!

I think I should come back and help you tame this jungle.

*I like the Secret Garden effect. But perhaps he's right, perhaps it's time to let in the light. He's as good as his word. Fifteen bin bags of ivy and rose cuttings later there is light!*

*Interview 10/08/2010*

# Carol

*A childhood in York; York City FC's first goal*

I suppose football was the reason I was born in York. Grandfather Mitchell, my dad's dad, originally from Scotland came to Durham as a miner in the early 1900's. He was a good footballer – so he escaped the pits as a young man to play for Newcastle in the late 20s early 30s. Grandfather had a little sports shop in South Shields. Then Leeds United signed him up and that's where he met Grandma. Her family were publicans from the West Riding. Their last pub was in Elland Road, Leeds. He moved to York City and holds the honour of scoring the first ever goal for York at Bootham Crescent, in a match that marked the opening of the ground in August 1932. He got a job to coach the Norwegian team so he and Gran eloped and married in Oslo. He came home in the war and was signed up by York City as a player-manager. They had Mitchell's sports shop on Bootham where the launderette is now. That's how the Mitchell leagues for young players got their name – they were sponsored by the sports shop. So that's how Dad came to be in York.

Mum was already living here not far away in Sycamore Terrace. Her father was a Kelly from an Irish immigrant family who were housed in Walmgate. Great grandfather, a policeman, lived round Tanner's Moat. Those houses are gone now.

They met at a dance in the De Grey rooms and did some of their courting at the Bay Horse in Marygate, which was a nice pub in the 50s and 60s. It had dances in the function room. They lived with Grandma first then bought their first house off Shipton Road. Dad and his brother later ran the sports shop and it moved into the city centre near King's Square. They were both keen sportsmen but Dad's activities were limited as he had a retina problem – he's partially sighted. He's just had a spell in hospital and I'm currently doing quite a bit of caring for him at his home.

I am the eldest of three girls and spent most of my childhood in and around Bootham and Clifton; Clifton Green with its shops and village atmosphere was quite a landmark for me. I had a lot of relatives round about. I went to Clifton Without Junior School and then to Queen Anne's. My first job was working in an office for British Rail. I didn't like it, though I stayed about five years. Then I got a chance to work at Elliott's Hotel in Sycamore Place. That was great. At that time it was *the* place to eat out and there was quite a buzz there. I loved it. Geoff, a retired padré, was a regular there; he and his wife Eileen, a bereavement counsellor, had lived in North Parade for a good while. He used to bring his Labrador. Geoff knew us as he had an interest in the property where Jo had his studio and where we lived for a time. He told us about a house for sale in North Parade. An elderly neighbour of his had died, so we negotiated for the house before it was even on the market. There were some fascinating people living there then. The Worsleys were still there then. I think he had been a secretary for Churchill and his daughter was a writer.

People wonder how I've managed to bring up three children in a small house with so little space, but we had the loft converted, and with Museum Gardens on the doorstep and the Homestead Park just a short walk away it wasn't a problem, though I wish Jo wasn't such a hoarder. The house is full of his photography stuff. I loved walking and took the children out a lot. Also my parents were nearby with a big garden. I nursed Mum there; she died of breast cancer.

I did my nurse training at the District Hospital. I worked nights when Becky was little then had a spell at the Hospice after Helen was born. I felt quite lonely in my marriage at that time. Things improved for a while after Jan was born; I worked at the Purey Cust Nursing Home near the Minster. For a while I had a fourteen-hour contract for a nursing bank agency then I was glad to move to being a practice nurse. I'm out at Elvington now. At that time it paid better wages than the hospital but things have changed now. Each practice can negotiate its own wages so sick pay and leave conditions have worsened. I have recently had to take a second job, working in a travel clinic in York.

I've been the main wage earner for some time. I found our hand-to-mouth existence quite hard at times – there were a couple of occasions earlier on through recessions when we were really struggling with a young family to look after. Financial problems definitely put a strain on the marriage.

All three children went to Easingwold Comprehensive School because Queen Anne's was a failing school at that time and eventually closed. It was OK for them because a group of local children went by bus each day; parents had to finance that.

Becky's mad about music and wants to be a DJ. She's interested in starting a music course at the Jam Factory – a studio in the Groves. Helen's the one who caused us a lot of anxiety as an adolescent but she's fine now. She's struggling to put together a full wage from a collection of part-time jobs – working at *Toys R Us* at the moment and doing an accountancy course. It will give her the equivalent of three A levels. Then she can apply for a decent job. She's much more focussed now.

I remember when they were younger the girls and Jan loved helping out at the street barbecues, running back and forth with supplies to Kath's house. Geoff and Jo would be in charge of the cooking. The millennium promenade meal was a lovely event too. Several houses were involved and we ended up at Geoff and Eileen's for a prayer at midnight. They moved out a couple of years ago as his health problems meant they needed to be in a bungalow. We've seen him heading for his local on a motorised scooter.

Our son Jan still goes back to Easingwold to ref and help the PE teacher which is good experience for him. He's done really well with his refereeing. He likes being called 'Sir'. At the moment he only has to travel to Leeds two days a week for his sports science course so it's cheaper for him to live at home. He would like to be a PE teacher eventually. He seems to have inherited a passion for football.

It's hard for Jo and I socially when things are so unsettled between us, but we were both glad to see our neighbour Joyce back in the street this summer for her 90th birthday.

*Interview December 2010*

# Joyce
*The last of the line*

*There is a For Sale sign outside number 10.*

*Joyce, in her late eighties, is always smartly dressed. She is meticulous about hats, and has a very independent mind under the hat. Though frustrated by her deafness and slightly stooped she is still sprightly and active so I'm surprised she's decided to move into sheltered accommodation. She's aware it is the worst possible time: a sudden recession has followed an unprecedented boom in the housing market. She is anxious; will she find a buyer in time to secure her chosen apartment? She knows exactly what she wants and intends to make this move while she is well enough to organise it herself. She's looking very smart today in a bright gold cardigan and amber beads, despite being in the process of sorting and packing. Facing me as I go in to the front room is a piano with its lid open and music on the stand. Beside it a slim-line screen announces 'Windows XP is shutting down'.*

My neighbour Ann passed this on to me. I was glad to have it because I don't have any hobbies. I use it for emails, and I like to ask it questions. It's a dreadful timewaster though. I used to go to a classical music appreciation group on Tuesday afternoons at Guppy's. [*Neal Guppy's Enterprise Club in Nunnery Lane.*] Such nice people but I don't always like the music. I think I have limited tastes. Neil Guppy selects and introduces the pieces. He's so well informed – has an encyclopaedic mind. Such a friendly group, but I had to give this up; it clashed with a lip reading class I needed; I was missing such a lot on TV.

I'm the last of my family line; I want to save my executors the pain of having to sort through the whole house. If I move now I'll have broken the back of the work. There'll be other benefits too.

*There's a glass-fronted bookcase clearly marked 'not for disposal'. The sofa, however, is piled with books that need a new home:* The Forsyte Saga, A Town Like Alice, *books about gardens and stately homes.* 'Do, please, choose something.' *I pick a slim millennium volume:* 2000 Years of York: The Archaeological Story.

Yes, I do enjoy reading, but I feel guilty. I should be doing something useful. I used to read when I was a voluntary steward at Fairfax House. [*A Georgian town house now owned by The Civic Trust.*] It was very quiet on my shift, rather a boring job really, but I always had a book with me. I did it for twenty-two years.

*We are interrupted by the chimes of a great clock. Joyce leaps up and points.*

I should have introduced you to Grandpa. He's the boss here. I inherited this ancient clock with an injunction that it *must* stay in the family. That posed a real problem. I have no family of my own and was an only child. In retrospect I realise Mother especially would have dearly liked a larger family and Father would have liked a boy to carry on the family name, but Mother was told another child could cost her life. Luckily I have found a cousin of Father's whose son would like the clock. There are other fine pieces of furniture that have been in the family for years. Great-grandfather was a cabinet maker.

I've been in York since 1954, initially in digs, and then I bought a wonderful house in Marygate, round the corner, St Mary's Cottage. I absolutely loved that house; it dated back to 1767. Mother joined me there in 1959. She lived to be 97. There had been dreadful floods in 1982. That house had flooded before, but it was the first time it had come up into the carpeted area of the house – there were no flood defences then. We looked for somewhere higher in the same neighbourhood – we liked the area so much. This was a lucky find. We moved to this present house in October 1982. I made detailed notes on all twenty-five prospective buyers of the Marygate house. I was determined to find someone who loved it too. The couple who bought it did a wonderful job of restoration and the people who followed improved the garden. Look, I've kept this estate agent's brochure. It resold two years ago at Auction for half a million pounds.

*Joyce, born in Nottinghamshire in 1920, left school in 1938 after her Higher Certificate with a scholarship to St James's, a prestigious secretarial college in Grosvenor Place, London.*

Only one scholarship was given each term. My parents would not have been able to afford the tuition fees. In the early days of their marriage they'd had no gas, electricity, or running water. They did pay for me to stay in the YWCA. Polio had delayed my studies for a year. I loved being in London; I was there two terms before the Blitz started. The College was evacuated into two branches; I was the only student to study in all three locations. Grosvenor Place was eventually flattened by bombs. By the time I returned home my parents had moved to Birkenhead. My father, a Post Office communications worker, had been promoted.

Through the Merseyside Blitz, in my spare time, I studied for the Chartered Institute of Secretaries at Liverpool College of Commerce. This I see as a big mistake in life. I found I was overqualified for the jobs I wanted. I didn't want responsibility, didn't want a job where I had to use my initiative. I'm a paper person not a people person; I haven't an ounce of empathy. Apart from the war period, when I worked in the finance office of Liverpool University, I always worked as a secretary.

My last post was with Munby and Scott, solicitors in Blake Street. I was personal secretary to the senior partner, John Shannon, who also happened to be chairman of the Civic Trust. [*He saved Fairfax House and the Observatory and restored the Mansion House. His funeral was held at York Minster 14/06/2010. He was 92.*] I enjoyed the Trust work much more than the legal business. When Mother became confused in her eighties I stepped down to part-time working to give her more time. She did handiwork in great variety: woodcarving, patchwork, all sorts; she made this cushion. I always copied what Mother did.

Mother would have started work in the First World War; she helped in the office of Father's blouse factory. He had previously been a commercial traveller but lost that job because he was vegetarian. He had refused a gift of a turkey from one customer at Christmas; his boss deemed this 'bad customer relations'. He probably regretted sacking him as he'd been a very successful salesman.

*Joyce brings in coffee and goes back for two paper napkins brought home from a café.*

I hate waste. I'm a Quaker; can I really call myself that when I'm not sure I'm a Christian? I think I'd describe myself as agnostic. But I like the silence. In the silence I can best do my seeking. I'm a seeker, not a finder.'

*Interview 25/09/08*

## Ann

*A flying start — batmen, bad dogs and choristers*

*Joyce's neighbour Ann is a petite figure with a sense of energy that belies the fact that she is about to retire. She has a quite a mischievous sense of fun which has stood her in good stead in the primary classroom. I've heard glimpses of Ann's story before over suppers with neighbours. I've always thought of her as a busy, methodical person and I'm surprised when she tells me:*

I'm quite an impetuous person. I got engaged to Stuart on the night we first met. It was 1968, a party at the officers' mess in Anglesey. He was a trainee fighter pilot. I was doing teacher training at Alsager's Cheshire — enjoying it, doing really well. I was told at the end of that term 'the sky is the limit, Ann!' but even as the words were spoken I knew I would leave. It was a difficult decision. I wept buckets — but it was right for him and his career. He functioned best if I was with him. We spent the first nine months of married life at RAF Conningsby, Lincolnshire. Our quarters backed onto carrot fields near Boston Stump. Can you imagine — I had a batman! [*A manservant in the armed forces — originally someone who looked after the bathorse or packhorse.*] He was used to batting for a Wing Commander; it must have been degrading for him to have to look after a young housewife. He taught me how to mix cocktails. He wrote out all his recipes for me. The station commander eventually realised what a treasure he was and took him off me, so he was back to the white gloves and the silver tray. My father had been in the Air Force — I'd grown up with all that.

It was a lonely existence for a young wife who was no good at bridge parties and coffee mornings. I had a Labrador dog that used to bring me rabbits with myxomatosis. I walked a lot; picked rosehips and hawthorn berries; watched the mist over the fen. Then we moved to RAF Chivenor, Devon – stayed in this ghastly haunted abbey at Barnstaple. The dog was terrified of it – used to chew his way out. The only secure place we could put him was the Priest's hole. Next it was Cotishall, Norfolk. We stayed on the Broads in a houseboat. I seem to remember the dog chewed through a sofa bed there! At least I could drive by then, but I was still no good at being a RAF wife.

Eventually we made our way to Wattisham, Suffolk. By now Stuart was with Treble One, an Active Fighter Squadron. It was a three-year contract, the longest time we'd been anywhere. Life changed a lot for us then. I was doing pupil teaching. We bought our own house but it needed doing up so Stuart stayed in the officers' mess and I was in digs, an old rambling house where the landlord was a diabetic with rotting feet. I hadn't realised the squadron didn't have my contact details; they'd rung the house and no one was in; so it was my mother who called – the only other contact they had – telling me to ring the station commander directly. I was shaking so much I couldn't dial. Stuart was missing over the North Sea. He had ejected before his plane ditched. Five of his friends had been lost in Lightning Aircraft in the 1970s. It had always been put down to pilot error. Fortunately Stuart was picked up alive and well. Later the plane was dredged up so they were able to establish that a mechanical fault had caused all these crashes.

It was when Stuart was a flying instructor at Linton-on-Ouse and Church Fenton that our family of three boys were born and while they were small I at last resumed my teacher training at York St John. It felt so good to be doing it again and such a bonus to have my own children to connect to the theory. It was heartbreaking to have to leave the oldest two, Ian and Jamie, behind when we got a posting to Saudi Arabia. We were there three years; Ross the youngest came with us for the first eighteen months and we got home to see the older ones every three or four weeks. Not enough, really. I was teaching at the British School in Riyadh. It was composed mostly of gifted children – a hugely challenging and hugely rewarding job. Then, suddenly, we were given forty-eight hours to leave. One of Stuart's students had crashed. It was the will of Allah that the plane should remain where it was; so no proper investigation was carried out and Stuart was deemed to be to blame.

I wrote to all the schools in the York area. We'd kept our family house near York fortunately. I found a job at Queen Margaret's teaching 9 to 11-year-olds. [*This is a fee-paying Independent Girls' School at Escrick just outside York.*] They were privileged children; when their junior department closed I moved to Copmanthorpe Junior School for a year – it felt good to be back in the real world.

It was much harder for Stuart to establish himself here. He really had taken a knock and he ended up going back to teach flying in the Middle East. So for ten years 1984 to 1994 I virtually brought the children up on my own. We were a good team. We expanded to accommodate Stuart when he was home on leave, a bit like an elastic band; saved up jobs to make him feel useful; but we were careful about the nature of the jobs after we'd been left without a kitchen worktop for three months at the end of one visit!

I was working at the Minster School by then and doing an Open University degree so I was a good role model for the boys; we all had some household chores and we were all studying. Life was good. But it was not so good for Stuart. It was getting harder to communicate with him; things were going badly wrong and we divorced in 1995. It was very sad. I still loved the man he'd been. A very difficult time for me. At the same time a very dear friend died of a massive heart attack on her way back from a concert we'd been to. She had been caring for her sick husband and I ended up supporting him till his death six months later. I was exhausted, juggling lots of things. Six months after that there was a knock at my classroom door, 'Could you step into the Head's office; there's someone here to see you.' The someone was from the Coroner's Office. 'A man has been found dead in York; we have reason to believe it is your husband.' It was indeed Stuart, by now my ex; he had had a massive heart attack. Devastating. No chance to say one's goodbyes.

It took a while to recover. I had a break at a place run by nuns in Whitby. After an interim period in a rented barn conversion I began to look for a new home. The minute I stepped on the doorstep of this house I had this really powerful feeling that it was absolutely right for me. I was relieved my offer was accepted. It was a time when gazumping was rife. I moved in February 1997. A funny thing happened when I chose a new paper, a William Morris one, for the hall some years ago. When the decorator finally reached the last of the old layers we realised that the original paper of 100 years ago was identical to the one I had just chosen, a design called *Compton*. I have to say I've enjoyed all this, choosing things, making decisions, making it my own. My latest addition here are curtains of another William Morris design called *Brer Rabbit*. I loved the fabric so much it's now in both sitting and dining rooms – it's perfect for this house which has been a haven for me.

I've loved teaching at the Minster school too, though it's my last term now. I've been there twenty-three years. About forty of the pupils are choristers. Leaving will be quite emotional; the school's been an extended family to me. I've been in this morning [*it's the middle of Ann's Easter holiday*] and sorted the rotten tubs outside the school. Who else will look after them now? I've brought home these resource boxes to sort out a new topic on Kenya. At the moment my room has a big display about the Nile from last term. Until three years ago I wrote a Nativity play each year. Great fun, but Christmas has been a lot less stressful since someone else took on that role! I shall miss the children especially.

I feel settled here, but so disturbing losing neighbours; I was shaken by Jill's death and it's such a shame Tim is moving, and possibly Teresa too, just when I would have more time for friends. I still miss Joyce, but visit her in her new apartment. Because of the RAF background I don't feel I have roots. I come from nowhere really; though from 8 to 18 we lived at Southend-on-Sea. Wonderful! I loved the sailing. I think I'll stay put now, though I do like travelling; I'm going to Italy next week. [*This became a longer holiday than planned. Ash from an unpronounceable Icelandic Volcano Eyjafjallajökull caused enormous disruption to air travel across western and northern Europe. Many planes were grounded for six days in April 2010.*]

I have a niece in Vancouver I'd like to visit when I retire and I'm planning a trip to India too. My sons are established in their careers: Ross is a management consultant over in America. He was married in the Minster and his daughter Maddie baptised there; Jamie is a medic – he's the one you met in the park with his little boy Henry; Ian is a surveyor in property management.

I think you and I should make a pact not to move! Although I have been thinking about VSO!

*Interview 07/04/2010*

*Ann held a party to celebrate Joyce's 90th birthday in July 2010.*

# John

*The reds and the blues – fishing, politics and jazz*

*John is a familiar figure walking by with his fishing rods. He introduced himself as secretary for the City of York Labour Party when I first moved here. Had I lived elsewhere, as an incoming member, I would just have had a welcoming letter.*

When I was fourteen, there was a choice to be made. This was Leicester education system: no eleven plus; everyone went to the same school till they were fourteen. Now, if I wanted to do 'O' levels I had to move to another school, or I could stay put and leave at fifteen. The choice was simple. I was staying put. Moving would mean wearing a purple uniform. A purple cap! A purple tie! I couldn't bear the thought of it. The teacher said to me, 'You're going to end up as a dustman!' The thing I'm proudest of – though I've nothing against dustmen – is that I ended up as an IT project manager.

I started work for Fox's Glacier Mints. They were taken over by MacIntosh in 1969. I was lucky; computing was just taking off then. I was the only one to move with the firm to Norwich because of my computing skills. Mind you, I'm not really interested in the technicalities of the computer, just its application, what it's capable of. I moved to York in 1975 after they in turn were taken over by Rowntree. Both Norwich and York are ancient cathedral cities but when I left in '75 Norwich was just beginning to become an overspill for London with firms moving their offices out there. Prior to that there were very few incomers. It seemed an insular place. It was the regional capital. There was no equivalent of Leeds nearby. So everyone came into Norwich to shop – it had an amazing shopping centre.

This is my first house. I didn't get it till 1983. I'd been in temporary accommodation when I first arrived, then lodged for a year with a friend, had six weeks in Haxby, then a year or so in St Mary's in a flat I didn't own. It's a difficult story really. My parents had kept a pub in Corby initially. They later moved to Wellingborough. It was a big culture shock for my mum when Dad moved from being a supermarket manager to a publican. She came from a fairly religious village background. As for me, I refused point blank to serve in the pub; that's not how I wanted to meet the public. They lived over the pub, so of course when Dad became crippled by arthritis he had to give up as landlord; suddenly they were homeless. I ended up buying them a house near Leicester, our home town, so all my own plans went out of the window; I had no money for a home of my own.

What drew me to this street? That's easy: it was the river! I needed somewhere relatively close to Rowntree's, good access to the Railway station – I don't have a car, never have had – and somewhere near the river. I'm a fisherman. I go fishing several times a week in the summer, anywhere between Scarborough Bridge and Rawcliffe. That's why in my current part-time job I try to do three half-days in the winter and only two in summer.

My work for the Labour Party serves both Central and Outer York, two elements created at the last boundary change. I'm also agent for our MP Hugh Bayley – his legal man, so my everyday tasks involve a lot of committee work, preparing agendas and reports. I think I have a logical mind, and though I haven't swallowed the rule book I do know chunks of it by heart. I used to deal with the post – maybe ten letters or so. Now with email and internet I can get up to thirty emails a day to deal with.

One of the most time-consuming things recently is that I have become, de facto, the landlord of the flat above their Holgate offices. A routine check from the fire brigade closed it down overnight. 'Where was the fire escape, the fire doors?' So I'm dealing with contracts and builders at the moment.

There'll be the extra work of the general election this summer, though no date has been announced yet. How hopeful am I? Well I think the Conservatives have lost the plot, but the fact that Labour have been in government for thirteen years is a problem. People are ready for change. There was a lot of public reaction to the war in Iraq – the Chilcott Enquiry is ongoing, probing the legality of the Iraq war. And then the MPs expenses scandal. Bayley is meticulous about these things. I feel strongly that MP's should be paid more, but equally strongly that they should have only one job.

*Michael Foot's death had just been announced. David Owen in paying tribute to him on radio remembered an inspirational speech in Plymouth when Owen was only 11. Was there, I wondered, a similar moment in John's life?*

Well, I was not a bit interested as a youngster even though Labour Party meetings were held at our house; but when I was 16, I came home from a cricket match one summer evening to be told, 'You've just been appointed branch secretary!' It was later, hearing a speech by Harold Wilson in 1964 at a big election rally in Leicester which converted me from someone with no interest to someone who was totally committed. I heard Foot speak some thirty years ago; I admired him in many ways, but didn't think he was the right man for Leader of the Party.

I also do half a day a week for the Samaritans. I'm not a listener – I'm their treasurer, do their admin. At one time I was a big badminton player, belonged to Rowntree's club and Action Sport. I have no car, but I used to get the bus out to walk on the moors. But arthritis means no badminton and my walking is reduced to a maximum of four miles.

My other interest is the blues; not acoustic stuff, electric guitar. There used to be a blues club at the Post Office in Marygate which I miss. I still go to Fibbers and the Duchess above it which used to be a snooker club. The Burnley Blues Festival is an annual event. And I'm going to Manchester Arena soon for the first time to see *Bad Company* – they were a *huge* band. I like live music to excite me.

I think this has been a fairly stable street; the only change is the amount of rented accommodation now. There's a young family with a baby next door. I don't suppose they'll stay if their family grows, these are quite small houses. The people across the road [*Jo and Carol*] they have been exceptional; their family of three have been brought up in the street. I don't know as many people as you for one reason or another. I'm quite a private person, but when I was younger and my parents were living in a cul-de-sac people got to know each other in the summer chatting across the gardens. We don't have that here. I wonder, when the book is published, if people will be surprised to find they've got a red in the street?

*Interview 03/03/2010*

## Teresa

*The fight for peace and equality; the battle with MS*

*I had joined Teresa, John's next-door neighbour, on the big anti-war demonstration in London on 15 February 2003. I couldn't believe that the Labour Party I had campaigned for was taking us into this war. A more recent trip with her to see Alan Bennet's* The History Boys *at Leeds Playhbouse had brought home again those issues of lives caught up in wars.*

I was determined to go on that anti-war march in London; I was hoping my legs wouldn't let me down. I have MS and it's so unpredictable. It was the slogan *Not in My Name* that most expressed my feelings. I thought it was an illegal war and my son James was already out in Iraq. He was in the paras. So neither I nor his wife ever knew exactly where he was. It's difficult coming to terms with the knowledge my son is a soldier. It helps that he sees himself as a peace-keeper. He's totally committed to what he is doing. I know the army is his life; he's in his element there. How many times do I ask myself, why couldn't he have been a teacher, or done outward bound work? When incidents are reported on the news, was he in the middle of that one or not? You just never knew. He had already survived Bosnia. I thought surely they'll have to listen if enough of us go to Hyde Park.

He survived Iraq and last year was featured in the local press when he got the Afghan medal for his work there as a medic. It's quite a good piece, but he wishes they'd said more about his team. At least at the moment he and his young family are safely in Germany.

James and Emma are children from a first marriage: I'd always wanted to teach; was on a teacher training course at York St John. Then, well, disaster: I suffered a typical Catholic girl's fate. I fell pregnant as a student – had to give it up; had two children quite close together. I was far too young. It was too close to my own girlhood when my sister Helen and I had shared the responsibility of bringing up a much-loved baby brother, after our mother's early death from cancer.

After my second child was born, post-natal depression led to a major breakdown, the end of my first marriage and the loss of custody of James and Emma. They stayed with their father who by then had a new partner. It was a grim, bleak time; my memory of it is quite murky.

After the teaching route failed, I followed Mother's footsteps into the Civil Service and moved south. I couldn't have done that hands-on caring that my sister Helen did as a health visitor, but I did want to do something that made a difference to people's lives. I like organisations; like a social context; I quite like rules and patterns; above all I like to think that what I do can change things for people.

Eventually I remarried and had Sarah. She was five when I first moved back north, a single parent by then, from Kent to Crayke. She had meningitis; my family wanted me nearer so they could help look after her. It wasn't until she was seven that I was able to introduce her to her half-siblings. She was delighted to discover them. I remember her asking, 'Have you any more surprises for me, Mummy?

Five years after my move north, just when things seemed to be going well I was diagnosed with multiple sclerosis. It was a lot to get my head round. Fortunately I don't have the primary form of MS which can lead to a rapid decline. My type – secondary progressive, which is relapsing and remitting – is less drastic but difficult in its unpredictability. You just don't know why or when it will be triggered or how long a relapse will last. Luckily I've had very few setbacks, lead a relatively normal life, even took up tennis again last year; but you do run out of energy. I'd loved village life in Crayke but what with commuting to Leeds and ferrying Sarah I was spending far too much time on the road. So I decided twelve years ago to move to the centre of York.

It was one of those chance things that brought me to this particular street: a good friend, Ann, had just moved here – she had been Sarah's primary teacher; later we both did an Open University social science degree. At her housewarming party I met Francesca and Trevor, neighbours who needed a bigger house for their growing family. They asked, 'Are you seriously wanting to move? Would you be interested in our house?' I was; and that's how it happened. I've not seen as much of Ann as I expected, we both lead such busy lives. We've managed a few holidays together. Last year it was Morocco. Fascinating, but I couldn't take the poverty. How can you haggle in bazaars with people as poor as that?

My daughter Emma has a baby daughter herself now. But she is mature, secure and has her own career. She says it's helped her understand what happened to me. It's meant a lot to me to be able to support her. It's uncanny that Emma is so like me in her reactions and responses to things. It can't be learned behaviour. When I visit her in Chester we take little Bea to the local Anglo/Catholic church – the angelus at the end of the service takes me right back to my own Catholic childhood.

I don't know what I believe now. Actually, *she laughs*, I think I could have been a nun, if I hadn't got caught up so early in a relationship! The Catholic Church left a huge mark on me; guilt mostly. I can't tolerate its excesses. I went to the Bar Convent but was drawn to the minimalism of the nearby Mount [*a Quaker Boarding School*]. I had a cousin there. Later the Mount School seemed the right choice for Sarah. Those were happy times; at weekends I wouldn't be sure how many girls were staying over at my house, we'd become the third boarding school; the girls used to call me 'Mrs K'. – The house was filled with laughter.

When Sarah went away to university it felt so lonely. I'm still close to my own siblings though our worlds are very different: my baby brother, Nigel, now based in London, is a successful actor. He had a great run in *The Thirty-Nine Steps* recently and visits when he's working in the north.

I spent a lot of time and energy being a governor at the Mount. I enjoyed the challenge: above all I enjoyed managing change. I have to admit I'm a workaholic. I still missed Sarah dreadfully. Later I got anxious when she became involved in modelling and media in London. Emma had at that time turned to teaching after doing law. 'Mum you'd love this!' she'd say, when she was reading literature; and I would, but it was too late for another career change for me. It was a relief when Sarah did a postgraduate teaching course. At least she has another option now. I'm so glad they all get on.

I've spent many years now in the Department for Work and Pensions. We've had more than our share of changes of minister this decade between reshuffles, scandals and resignations: Alan Johnson, David Blunkett, James Purnell – I've lost count really, and they all had to be briefed! I'm a project manager. One project was to get Pensions' literature translated into plain English. Quite a task! Luckily I did have the chance to study again; the Civil Service supported me through an OU degree and an MA. I did research into the impact on children of being part of a family living on benefits. It was a big surprise getting the MBE. We had a great day out in London; both the girls and Helen were there. Lots of excitement about choosing hats! Then I borrowed one from Jill. Very special. Long time ago – 2001.

This new job in Equality and Diversity is just what I wanted. Very exciting. It connects with my previous involvement with the Child Poverty Action Group in York and the setting-up of a Minister for Women and a Children's Commissioner. I'm enjoying it so much. That's the good news; but most of my work now is in London. Sooo – I'm thinking of moving south again.

The desire not to spend so much time commuting is driving me out in the same way as it drew me in. There are so many unknowns in a move. I've had a really supportive consultant in York. I do hope I'm doing the right thing. I think it is the right time to rejoin village life. Isn't it strange, I realise when I've been looking in Kent I'm trying to replace the cottage I had in Crayke! I do find the idea of London exciting. You must come and visit me.

*Interview 25/02/2010*

*I promised; but thought at the time it wouldn't be the same as just popping down the street for a chat. I would miss Teresa. She has such good humour, such a positive outlook. We've had a lot of good times together including holidays and theatre trips since we met at one of Kath's barbecues. I would miss sitting in her light, bright conservatory kitchen, with its pretty blue china and its fresh flowers. I remember it was built for Sarah's 21st party. Recently this uncluttered space has sprouted tepees and toys since the arrival of Thomas, the first of four grandchildren, and Nellie, her brother's first child. They've given her such a lot of pleasure, a lot of fun. Teresa's idea of heaven is having them all together in one big family gathering.*

*Postscript. December 2010*

*Teresa's house sale fell through; she lost a dream home she'd found in Kent. This set back necessitated a much longer commute and the change of government brought a hugely increased pressure of work and a fear that the new Equality Bill, on which Teresa had been so pleased to work, would be unpicked. The stress of all these things together led to an MS relapse followed by a bout of pneumonia. My youthful, workaholic friend was looking at early retirement offers.*

## Vera

*North Yorkshire Moors ranger; a childhood in Southern Rhodesia*

*Vera is another distinctive figure in the street, setting off or returning home on her bike, safely helmeted or walking out purposefully, rucksack on back, a warm squashy purple-brimmed hat framing her face. There are often posters in her window for Christian Aid events and today for* Clear Exchange *a play at the Riding Lights Theatre. It's a bitterly cold day; there's been yet another sprinkling of snow, so it doesn't surprise me when she answers the door in her fleece and fingerless shocking pink gloves.*

I can date my arrival in the street quite precisely. It was October '87. My mother had died that year. I'd shared a house with her at Fulford. It was far too big for me on my own. We were there partly because it was relatively near my work. I taught science at Queen Margaret's out at Escrick. I wanted to move nearer the centre and a bonus was living in the parish of St Olave's, which I enjoy. We'd been in Fulford since 1981. I can place that quite precisely too – it was the year Charles and Diana married; we were watching it on TV as we finished the packing.

No, I didn't grow up in York. My parents were German refugees before the war. I was actually born in India – in an area which is now part of Pakistan. Difficult to separate actual memories from photos and stories. We were on the move a lot. My father had eventually joined the British Army out there. At the end of the war he thought, where do we go now? If they'd come to England he could have got a job, but there was no housing. Australia was a possibility; there would have been housing, but no job. Mother was still in touch with a friend who had emigrated to Southern Rhodesia well before the war. She

103

told them there would be both housing *and* work out there. So they said 'Let's try it.' They stayed for thirty years.

The longest I was anywhere in one house as a child was during my schooldays in Southern Rhodesia from 1947-57. I don't think I took in much about the politics or the landscape initially. I remember we arrived at the end of a school year. *My* greatest concern was how I would get on at school. I'd be 7 then and had not had much in the way of formal tuition. I think Mother had taught me my times tables. Of course the schooling was all segregated, separate schools for Blacks, Coloureds, Indians and Whites. We lived in Bulawayo, the second largest city – wide tree-lined streets and beautiful turn-of-the-century buildings. I'd lived in India and Malaya so was already used to living amongst people with different coloured skin and there were servants around as before. Father became a lawyer, had his own practice and Mother became his secretary. In his business and personal life Father treated everyone as equal. I can see this now but didn't realise then how unusual this liberal attitude was in that environment.

It wasn't until the late Fifties early Sixties that the black-led ANC became more active seeking political control for the black African majority. A new University College of Rhodesia and Nyasaland had been built – the only place where people were educated together. I remember a lot of people raising objections, but it hadn't been going long enough to be sure of its standards so I came to Britain to go to university in 1958.

I read Chemistry at Manchester. What a shock England was! Especially the weather! Awful – and the dark nights in winter. I'd had a brief holiday over here with my parents, but basically I was finding my way about on my own then. Luckily I was in a hall of residence. Then I spent four years in Toronto doing a PhD in physical inorganic chemistry. I still have good friends from that period. By the time I came back to Rhodesia to teach, Ian Smith had made his Unilateral Declaration of Independence (1965). The British Government's attitude, of course, was 'no Independence without Majority rule'. Things became quite difficult. Now Mugabe cannot accept any whites to be true Zimbabweans – such a shame. I remember one girl at school whose family had lived there for five generations even then.

So after seven years in the Mission school I found a job near York and began teaching at Queen Margaret's. I eventually became Head of Department, but was shunted for a while into admin, in charge of timetabling and exams, which wasn't me at all, so I took early retirement in 1994.

One of the things I knew I wanted to do from the word go was to be a voluntary ranger on the North York Moors. This is predominantly weekend work, but I also belong to a Tuesday group doing maintenance jobs: cutting down trees, clearing paths, planting, gravelling. Do you remember the flash flood at Bilsdale in 2005? That left a lot of debris, which we helped to clear – such an enormous torrent in such a short time. I work mainly on the western side. An old mill near Arden Hall got completely silted up. That was quite satisfying working to see it restored.

I used to work for Oxfam, initially from a depot near Rowntree Park – I drove a van to empty the book and clothing banks; the donations were then sorted and distributed to the various outlets. A couple of young lads from a local hostel, where youngsters were being supported and trained to cope on their own, were assigned to work with me to do some of the heavier lifting. They were lovely and still greet me warmly when I see them in town. It was when that depot closed I worked at Goodramgate where I sorted books. But goodness! So many changes of management systems and criteria for selecting and pricing. The last straw was when the possibility of recycling/ selling elsewhere was vetoed. It was 'sell them here or pulp them'. I thought this outrageous, put on my hat and coat, and left.

I'm still a bridge player, both at New Earswick and the York club on Holgate. Thank heavens Scarborough Bridge has reopened. It's much quicker that way, though there's no lighting at the moment. It never worries me walking in York at night, though I know things do happen. A friend was mugged coming home from church in broad daylight on a Sunday. I did worry about the number of break-ins to cars parked at the end – the smashed glass about. There was a real spate of that, but things are better now.

Also, I'm in demand as a bell-ringer. It takes quite a while to become competent. It's not dangerous but you should work with someone who knows what's what when you're learning. Stories of people crashing into the rafters are apocryphal. The worst damage I've seen is rope burns on the palm of hands. We train people, but then they find it too much of a regular commitment. My first call is to St Olave's, but other churches import people for weddings and funerals. Then there's the Ramblers; I'm the York Group Secretary. And I play Scrabble with the U3A (University of the Third Age) twice a month. The first session is more social, you can look things up, it's at Bishopthorpe Village Hall. The second is run on club rules and rotates round people's houses. This week it's at Fulford. Would you like to come?

*I did go and was made welcome but found it too serious for me, still miss my regular social sessions with Jill.*

I've lived in York almost as long as I was in Rhodesia. After my early nomadic life I feel settled. This is home now.

*Interview 22/02/2010*

*Postscript 14/07/2010*
*Vera called on me in July sporting a York Volunteer Archaeologist's T-shirt.* 'Oh yes, it's one of my regular things.'

*I wonder how many days in the week for all these pursuits? She'd been digging at Hungate. This area to the east of York city centre, adjacent to the River Foss, is now the site of the biggest ever archaeological dig in York city centre uncovering 2,000 years in the life of York, showing what Viking life was like, uncovering part of a 1,700-year-old Roman cemetery, and revealing how people used the land in medieval times.*

We started on the Victorian level; we knew exactly the number of the house on a named street, Haver Lane. We met an old man who'd been a child there. 'This was my house,' he said, 'my sister lived over the road.' – Wonderful!

*I asked Vera about the much-publicised find of the bones of Roman Gladiators.*

Well there were an awful lot of bones. I feel they've picked the ones that fit the theory; though most people agree there must have been an amphitheatre here.

*Before she left I asked about her former Filipino neighbours. I had met some of them two years ago when they had invited me to join a party. I knew they were interested in being included in the story of the street, but the house was standing empty. Vera gave me a forwarding address.*

*Vera also left an invitation to her birthday party in St Olave's Church Hall. How kind. And there they all were – the bell ringers and bridge players, the diggers and delvers, the ramblers and scrabblers, even a friend from her time in Canada, and some neighbours, all wishing her well at 70.*

## Kirsty and Simon

*For a long time Japan was 'home'*

*Like Vera, Kirsty and Simon had very itinerant childhoods.*

**K:** We met as pupils of the International School in Japan! I'd been born in Canterbury, but not there long; we were always on the move. My dad, who as a boy had lived on a farm in the Lake District, became a biochemist and worked for a company who sent him all over the world. Our family went to Japan in 1991 and I was there full time for eight years, but travelled back there for my holidays from uni for another two years. 'Going home' meant going back to Japan. I was just 15 then when we first met. Simon's dad also had a job which involved a lot of travel. They were living in Tokyo for the last two years of his schooling when he was 17. It was a good school. We made many lasting friends there. I'd studied Japanese as part of the International Baccalaureate. I feel more a sense of connection with Japan than anywhere.

**S:** We've been in the house two years and really like it here. The previous occupants had only been in eighteen months and I think they had spent the whole time renovating the place then needed to move on as she'd had a new baby. So we've benefited from their DIY, which is just as well, as DIY is definitely not my thing! We like the mix of modern furnishings with the original Victorian features.

*The room has polished wooden floors; they're sitting on an aubergine sofa with a bold modern image of New York above them.*

It's friendlier here. So this is just a progression up the property ladder. Before that we had a flat in Lawrence Street.

We didn't really know our neighbours there. We had no previous connections to York. It all happened by chance. Kirsty came first.

**K:** Yes, I'd left London to join Simon who'd taken his first job back in Dublin where he grew up. I worked there for a year, but started to apply for graduate programmes in England. I'd found one with Norwich Union (as was, Aviva now) and was in Norwich for all of three days before we were relocated to York! That's nearly six years ago. It's great for me because I can just stroll down the river to work. Simon commutes to Leeds.

**S:** It's an easy train journey. Especially now I can walk to the station via Scarborough Bridge since it reopened. [*At the time of the interview Simon who now works for Aviva too, was working for a building society in Leeds.*] I deal with commercial loans, but it's not easy for businesses to get loans in the current climate.

**K:** All our friends and social life are here now. Thirty of us were all starting at Aviva at the same time on this programme on a weeklong induction; many became close friends. Because that already existed we haven't made many friends in the street.

**S:** Do I still feel my roots are in Dublin? Well, I still feel a sense of patriotism, still shout for the Ireland teams. I've told Kirsty if we have children and they're sporty they would have to play for Ireland! The economic situation there would make it quite difficult to move back. There was a strong sense of community. My grandma, for example, lived in an area where terraced housing went all round a square and people knew each other. I think my affection for that place is one of the reasons I was drawn to live in a terrace like this. But when she died I was sad to see hers was the last house in it to still be a family home; the others had all been turned into flats. I still have family connections there; my sister lives there, and I keep in touch with a few friends. My own parents are in Bahrain at the moment and I have a sister in America.

**S:** I loved Japan. I had a lot of freedom there because it's such a safe country. It gets under your skin. Kirsty and I had been friends a while and started going out together just before we were going to uni. By then our choices were already made; Kirsty had a place at Cardiff to do Business Studies. I was going to Goldsmiths to do Anthropology. I got to know National Express coaches quite well! I felt a big city like London would be a way of continuing the adventure of Japan. Difficult at first because I didn't know anyone, but yes, it was exciting. There was an interesting ethnic mix and a large Afro-Caribbean community in that area of London. Four of the five people I was sharing with to start with were not from the UK. I especially enjoyed my final year; by then I was sharing with a friend from Japan.

**K:** This was a difficult period for me. It felt scary going halfway across the world to university. I was only 17. Then when I got there I found I was classed as an international student as my parents had no property in the UK at that time, so I was housed with people from very different backgrounds, mostly Europeans. Having been out of England so long I also had none of the cultural referents that the other English students had either; I knew nothing of the TV programmes they'd been watching – felt completely out of it. Many of our friends have their biggest group of friends from their university days; for us it's our school friends who have lasted.

**K:** Simon and I both did our Masters in Market Management in Surrey.
  *Simon acknowledges there is absolutely no connection between anthropology and market research: he just hadn't a clue what he wanted to do at the end of his degree.*

My Masters followed on more naturally from Business Studies. How did I get into that? Well I didn't enjoy school till the last two years but suddenly found myself enjoying that course. Now I specialise in customer strategy which involves interviewing a lot of older people; it's been fascinating finding out what your generation get up to in their retirement. Many wonder where they found the time to work!

**K:** My mother was a secretary, working in the same firm as my dad. When we lived in Switzerland she became a kindergarten teacher, but she didn't work after our move to Japan in 1991. My parents are living in Singapore now, but Dad has bought a property in the Lake District, where he spent his childhood, in anticipation of his retirement. He took great delight in showing it to *his* 92-year-old dad. In some ways I envy his sense of roots.

But of course we do have an important connection with York now – it's where we got married, just before we moved into the street a couple of years ago. The ceremony was at Bedern Hall, the reception at the Churchill Hotel and we had a whole table for friends from Japan and one for the Dublin family and friends.

**S:** We've been in York for six years now. Do I have itchy feet? No, York's a good place to be – we're well content with it.

*Interview 08/03/10*

## Janet and Stewart

*A lifetime in North Yorkshire; a family abroad.*
*Coastal erosion, the end of the Holbeck Hall Hotel.*

**J:** I love seeing the sunlight filtering through the windows when I walk through the Minster in the early morning or evening. *Janet works three days a week in the Minster shop.* I've always been in retail; did Saturday jobs as a schoolgirl. It's quite a long day 10-6.30 in summer. Charges were introduced at the Minster a few years ago. We weren't really happy, but they don't get a government grant, and not enough voluntary donations. York residents, of course, can get a pass. We meet some interesting people and tend to act as an unofficial Tourist Information point. It was mainly American visitors when I first started. They came here out of their B & B's early, then headed off for Edinburgh or the Lakes, though we did our best to encourage them to see the Dales and the Moors. The Americans seem to have dwindled; there are a lot more Chinese visitors now.

I grew up in Guisborough. Stewart and I met at school in Middlesborough. He is a civil engineer, semi-retired now – still does some consultancy work. He's busy getting some papers ready for a meeting. We lived at Danby for thirteen years. Jonathan would be 7 and Clare just 3 when we went there. She still talks about the dinner lady, Mrs Baxter, at the little village school who cooked the meals from locally sourced products. Just before Clare left, the government insisted on meals coming in pre-packed. She was gutted. It's come full circle now with Jamie Oliver's school dinners initiative. I'm glad they grew up in the country where they could play out safely, though it was a long journey for them from Danby to the senior school in Whitby. They got the bus just after eight, and weren't home till half five.

Stewart commuted to Teeside; he didn't mind; it was a lovely journey. I worked at Danby Lodge in the North Yorkshire Moors National Parks Visitor Centre. They leased this beautiful building which had been Lord Downe's shooting lodge. It had an exhibition centre; school parties came, and there was an office for the Rangers. A great place to work.

After this we lived for a while near Scarborough at West Ayton. Stewart had had quite a stressful and challenging time there. He needed a move and found employment with North Yorkshire County Council. He started off in the Northallerton office so we let the house out to a couple of law students for a year; the commuting was grim but he eventually got a transfer to the York office.

*Stewart who has joined us now comments:*

**S:** I shall never forget that period. It was 1993 when the Holbeck Hall Hotel near Scarborough slipped into the sea, on my watch, as it were. I was Deputy Director of Technical Services for the council at the time. I had a responsibility for coastal erosion. A million cubic metres of material had fallen and left a huge hole. Deeply distressing for the people who'd lost their homes and businesses, and for others left stranded who'd lost every bit of value in their properties overnight. What's more, the poor folk were worried about what would follow. Would there be further landslides? It was distressing for me because there were immediate allegations that the council were to blame and a court case followed.

**J:** It was a blazing hot May. I remember you came back with your forehead burnt.

**S:** I was more concerned about the heat of the media; there were vans everywhere bristling with antennae. So we had not only the challenge of stabilising the cliff, but the full barrage of the press to deal with. Such a graphic incident made not just local headlines but national and international news. I was used to dealing with the public and press, but this was beyond anything that had happened before. The politics of it all got me down in the end. I felt it would have been easy to have been scapegoated by councillors. It was difficult to know who to trust. Now as a consultant I'm called in to do a technical job; you have a client buffer between yourself and the public.

Now there's some time for leisure. I'm a keen cyclist, and we keep in touch with our friends from North Yorkshire. Once a month I meet up for a walk with old colleagues – 'the old gits' Janet calls us, but they're good company. One guy is 78 and still going strong. Of course we have a sit down at the pub and catch up with news. Janet and I have time now to swim and go to City Screen cinema.

**J:** It's sad we can't spend more time with the children as both families are living abroad. Clare went out to the Cayman Islands [*in the Caribbean*] this December. She actually left while we were visiting Jonathan in Australia. Her partner got this job offer he just couldn't refuse. She'd been there five years ago and liked it, but that was before she had Gracie and Wilf. It's a limited period contract though and I'm *sure* she'll come back. She loves North Yorkshire. She's into interior design. She did a course with Mulberry Hall – was down in London for a while. But we don't think Jonathan will come back; they seem to have settled in Australia. They've been there four years now. My mum says it is history repeating itself. My brother emigrated in his twenties to New Zealand and we see little of him. He came back a year or so ago to see Mum – spent a week with her. But so sad for her; he made it clear it would be his last visit. She's in her late eighties now. She's lived in York for twenty-five years, though she came from Durham originally. I see her each week.

**S:** Our son, Jonathan is a pharmacist. He trained in Nottingham. He did some work for Boots, but they expected him to become a manager of one of their centres. He didn't want to do that; he wanted still to be doing pharmacy and dealing with the public; that's why he did locum work. It is the same in many lines of work. Your early years are more fulfilling – promotion tends to move you out into admin and management.

*When Stewart goes off to his meeting, Janet takes me into the kitchen. She shows me a little gallery of photos and art work from the grandchildren she misses so much. There are pictures of her son's three ranging from 6 to 10 years old on an Australian beach. And one of Gracie in her last English school photo at Baldersby St James before they went to the Caymans. What a coincidence. My aunt taught at this village primary near Ripon for two decades or more. My brother was sent there for a week in October 1947 because I was being born. He learned about compost heaps and potato harvests.*

**J:** At least we can email, text, and once a week we Skype them so we still feel connected. But it's lovely to see them in person. We spent three weeks out in Australia this December. Great, but it took a week to get over the jet lag!

We don't have close friends in the street but we know quite a few people to speak to. I miss seeing the two old ladies along here. I always had a word when they were going shopping with their trollies; they kept sprightly for a long time. Old Mrs Dunne died; she was a very trendy 90-year-old, very fashion conscious, she always had a hat on. Hilda sadly is in a home now; she had lost her husband when they were on holiday in Spain. She had a son in his sixties up in Scotland but he had a stroke and she was devastated when her grandson died. The two ladies had lived here all their married lives.

We didn't know our neighbour Jill well but thought she was a lovely person to live next to. It seemed very quiet last year when the house was empty; not that she was noisy, but we used to hear her talking to friends in the garden. You were there often weren't you? She liked the radio and music on in the kitchen; we used to hear the French *chansons* over the garden wall, I think her friend had given her them. I could have sworn I saw him in York the other day, but Stewart said I must be mistaken as he was sure he came from Cornwall.

*I explain that 'Jill's friend' was 'my brother' and he had moved up from Cornwall when he retired last year and is now living at the other side of York.*

**J:** Oh! I'd no idea. That explains a mystery then. I was right.

*Interview 04/03/2010*

## A retrospective. Jill
*A Russian spy?*

My friendship with Jill began when she arrived in this street two years after I first came to live here. Rummana had thrown a party to say goodbye to Julia, and by chance it was able to provide a welcome for Jill too. She was a tall, elegant, blonde, blue-eyed woman with a very warm smile. She and I knew we'd be friends from that very first meeting, though in many ways we were opposites. She was a very homely person, loved baking, specialised in a walnut loaf and made beautiful clothes for herself and her family; everything from walking trousers to long evening skirts, though she very rarely wore skirts. She loved fabrics and enjoyed going to the markets and charity shops to have a rummage. Jill had three cats to my one when she first arrived. She belonged to the ramblers but when we first met she was much more energetic than me. I couldn't manage the 12-14 mile 'A' walks she did with ramblers but we often set off, sometimes with Sue, for more modest walks that were within my range. I remember a lovely day near Kirkham Priory, sitting in the evening sun at the pub afterwards. Later arthritis curtailed her walking to the point where only her bike allowed her to get into town.

We sometimes teamed up for suppers with Ann and Teresa: Jill did a fantastic bean stew. (All four of us had a son called James! Mine spent some time here when I first moved and Jill frequently joined the two of us for supper.) Jill had a much wider circle of friends in York, having lived in the city for many years. I gradually got to know some of them and enjoyed their friendship too. What was great was having this easy no-need-for-ceremony ability to call in on each other on days when there was no family around and not much else happening. It was great sharing simple things, cups of tea, walks, suppers, photos of holidays and eventually grandchildren. There were not many winter weeks that didn't find time for a game of Scrabble, a friendly version where we were allowed to look words up. Our joint score was usually well over 500. We'd look out for each other on our return home from holidays to share our stories. I remember her excitement coming across with the news of the arrival of her first grandson. And much later a Christmas Eve dinner when she was bubbling over with the news of her youngest son's engagement to Abi, a stunning red-headed dancer.

Jill was a part-time special needs teacher at Limetrees, a hospital unit that catered for children and adolescents with a range of mental health problems. She would never discuss individual cases but I was aware that some pupils had eating disorders, were anorexic or bulimic or self-harmers. Jill was self-deprecating about her work. She might only have a handful of pupils at any one time, but it took a special sort of person to provide contact with their schools and families and provide for their educational needs across a range of subjects while they were being assessed and treated. She would sometimes come round hunting for things, 'Have you anything on Anne Frank? I've someone doing that for GCSE. Do you have a video of *All My Sons*? What do you make of this poetry anthology?'

I remember Jill telling me she'd written to Mark Haddon about his *The Curious Incident of the Dog in the Night Time* which had helped her understand Asperger's, and how kind he'd been to reply. Just at that time I was trying to book him as a speaker for the *Riverlines* event series which I ran for York St John at City Screen's basement bar. Jill regularly supported these and often brought other friends too. I had a party here for her 60th birthday. I remember planting up window boxes for her yard. Jill's mum, who'd had a career as a physiotherapist, was a keen gardener but

Jill hadn't inherited her green fingers and was delighted when I brought plants.

She suspected they would close down this educational liaison work after her retirement. She was very anxious about retirement – how would she fill the time. She was hoping my brother would retire too from his poetry publishing business in Cornwall, but he wasn't ready at that time.

I had introduced Jill to my brother when he was staying here for Christmas 2000. Harry had lost his wife earlier that year. It had been a long, happy and productive marriage. He and Jill really took to each other and despite the huge journey from Cornwall to York became partners. They spent the following Christmases in York. Harry kept a second-hand bike in Cornwall for Jill so that she could explore the steep wooded lanes in the Tamar Valley when she visited. It seemed very strange at first having my brother staying across the road, but Jill became family. She and Harry often went for a few days between Christmas and New Year to stay with his lovely daughter Hannah and his grandsons, my great nephews, in Norwich.

In between her trips to Cornwall she and I still had our outings to the coast and to events in York. But she suffered a series of health problems: a hip replacement, a cancer, then a new knee. Each time it looked as if she'd made a good recovery. Because of time in hospital and earlier mobility problems she'd missed out on holidays, and by 2008 she was desperate for a break. In the past she had holidayed in France with my brother, Brittany, Normandy, Collioure, but he was grounded just then, waiting for two new knees himself.

At this point I had just retired and was able to take an early spring holiday. Jill was keen to join me at my favourite destination – a sleepy village in the Aveyron where my close friends Chris and her husband Jo have a second home. I've visited nearly every year since 1996. Jill had seen photographs and was quite envious of Teresa's visit some years before. It's my idea of paradise. I was looking forward to introducing her to the area: the high Causse country, the steep ravines, the Bastide market towns. Jill, a keen Francophile, was excited but she said she could only stay the first week, she'd have to get back to look after her mum.

The month before we go she starts feeling sick, assumes it's something she's eaten. But it doesn't go away. Two days before our departure she goes to the doctor. He finds a puffy liver. She'll need a scan. I suddenly have a sickening feeling too. I guess what this must mean. I have already lost three close friends to cancer. But she still wants to go to France anyway and have the scan when she gets back. So on the first of May we set out.

She loves it, the leafy lanes, the masses of irises, the view from the garden, the double chiming of the church clock, the clopping of horses past the terrace, the local cats, the fresh strawberries and asparagus in the markets. We have a ride out to see the towns built into the cliff above the winding Lot valley. We stop in one little town at a 'vide-greniers' (an emptying of the attics) which is just her thing. We try the local auberge. She admires the tablecloths, chats fluently to Madame; but she can eat hardly anything. It's worse than I thought. She has headaches. We take things easy. Despite all this she beats me at Scrabble and is elated. I can see she's going down rapidly. She doesn't want me to call the doctor. 'Do you think it's a touch of sunstroke, Mum?' her son had asked on the phone. She is still talking about looking after her mum when she gets home.

I arrange for her to have wheelchair assistance at Stansted airport. She is met by her sons. She's is delighted to be there in London with them and two of her grandchildren. One month later in a packed St Olave's Church her funeral service was conducted by her nephew, Daniel. The boys say goodbye to a special mum who had seemed so vibrant and energetic only weeks before. Her oldest son Ross and his Indian wife Seema who live in Cheshire had recently had their first long-awaited child. One of my last memories of Jill is of her lying on a hospital bed cradling this little one. She was so good with little ones. My granddaughters loved seeing her on their visits here.

Harry also gives an address at the service. He explains how well she catered for his sartorial needs from Oxfam; but how many, he wonders, knew of her alter ego as a Russian spy? They laugh when he says she could detect a Russian speaking voice at 500 metres. Jill, a keen linguist, had recently joined a Russian conversation group, and was keen to find new members.

But it wasn't till she died that I fully realised how much my sense of well-being here had depended on the warmth of her friendship. I think she'd become the sister I never had. My relationship with the street changed after Jill was gone. I was haunted by the sight of her riderless bike in the forecourt.

Jill's sister Sue, with whom she was very close, has thankfully kept in touch. I was amongst friends invited to the English celebrations of their daughter's wedding which had taken place out in Tunisia that summer. Sue and her husband Ron had expected to have Jill with them when they went out there for the wedding, but it was not to be.

The following spring it was Jill's youngest son Jim's wedding in the crypt of St Paul's Cathedral in London. Many of Jill's friends from York were invited. A blue teasel design from her recent art work was used on the invitation and place settings and the theme reflected in the wedding flowers.

Jim now owns the house across the road. I remember Jill warning me when he first came home after his music studies in Liverpool, 'I'm afraid he has drums!' Reading Jim's story, now I know why she was so worried!

It must have been hard to let go of the house. Belongings speak so much of the owner; such a lot of fabric and clothes and china; posters and prints from France; cat ornaments and cards. It looked as if Jill was about to walk back in – her glasses out – the piano opened – her bag of crocheting – her new art materials. But eventually the time came.

# Jim

*A life in music; from drums to the night garden*

I first walked through the door of Mum's house in North Parade when I was 19. I had just returned home from my first year at Liverpool Institute for Performing Arts. Mum had recently moved from a huge house in St Paul's Square. Neither I nor my brothers were around to help. There must have been so much stuff, a great deal of it mine! She would have had friends around, but she must have done a lot on her own. But that was my mum, independent and strong. I guess she'd learnt these qualities whilst bringing up three sons by herself!

Our family came to York in 1984 from Riccall, a small ex-mining village just outside of York, where I had lived since I was born. We moved into a Victorian house with four floors and a cellar in the Holgate area of York. At that time St Paul's Square had a number of derelict houses. Now it's picture perfect, one of the most desirable parts of York to live. Unfortunately Mum and Dad split up not long after our arrival in York, and later divorced. When Ross and Craig left for university in the early 90's Mum and I rattled around this huge house. I took it upon myself to occupy every possible room with musical instruments or gym equipment and held multiple parties. In 1999 when I left for university it was time for Mum to downsize. Her search for a new home began.

I do remember her excitement when she told me, 'I've found a house I love!' When I came home from university and saw it for the first time I could see it was absolutely perfect for her, the street and the house were just right. It overlooked St Peter's playing fields in a quiet street – a great location for Mum so close to the centre of York as she'd often make three or more trips into town on just one day! She had a choice of routes: through the Museum Gardens, along the river or down Bootham. Mum would frequently be seen pedalling her way through the streets of York. She loved the markets. If she could, she would have cycled everywhere. York is one of the few cities in the UK that you can get around solely by bike.

Mum's friendly, generous nature and the welcoming community of North Parade meant she quickly made new friends in the street, and being so near the centre of York she could keep in touch with all her previous friends and neighbours too. It was as if she had lived there all her life.

Mum's talent was languages; she spoke French fluently. Her degree in Leeds in the 60s had specialised in Russian and she also spoke German and Spanish well. Had things been different she would like to have worked abroad, perhaps for the Civil Service. But she began her career in secondary education teaching foreign languages.

Later, for many years, she had a specialist teaching job at Limetrees Hospital on Shipton Road. She didn't talk about it much other than to remind me how lucky I was, but I could see it was a demanding job. A testament not only to her teaching skills but to her patience too.

I now live in London with my wife, Abi, who is an actor. I make my living as a professional composer and arranger, something I attribute in no small way to Mum. Not because she was a musician, although she did play a bit of piano, but because she was so supportive of everything I did. She encouraged me to play the piano as well as the drums and drove me to rehearsals and lessons. It was Dad who sent me for my first drum lessons when I stayed with him in London – I think I was about 11 or 12 at the time – but he was more sceptical of my chosen career because it wasn't something he understood.

My older brothers, who spent more time with Dad when

they were growing up, have careers closer to his. Craig, like Dad, became a chartered surveyor. He went into the world of finance; Ross, the eldest, helped establish one of the UK's earliest and most successful internet service providers. They've both always been keen on anything that has an engine! I didn't seem to acquire this same obsession. However, over time I have developed an interest in fast and expensive cars; too bad I decided to become a composer! Dad, who was awarded the OBE as Vice Chancellor of the University of Greenwich, stood by my decisions and towards the end of his life seemed happy that I was making a living doing what I loved.

My musical life began on the drum kit much to the annoyance of the other occupants of St Paul's Square. North Parade should be very glad that by the time Mum moved into the street I had sold my drum kit! I terrorised the whole square with my drumming. With band rehearsals every weekend. I'm surprised we weren't chased out! Actually we were occasionally threatened with legal action. Once a chap came round and offered to soundproof our cellar! Being the horrible teenager that I was I didn't care, I practised hour after hour until I left for uni. Our band, 'The Great Uncle Tonies', consisted of myself and three of my best friends who I still see on a regular basis. Our greatest claim to fame was winning York's 1995 Battle of the Bands competition!

During my first year in Liverpool I gradually moved away from the drums, pop and jazz of my youth towards writing and arranging music – a much better, and more lucrative, career option. I miss playing the drums but I don't regret my decision.

My professional career began at Metropolis Studios in 2000 when I got the illustrious job of night security man, which was the main route for aspiring engineers and producers at the time! I wasn't too sure what I wanted to do until a well-known record producer came up to me and said he had a string section coming in to record a 'Sheba' cat food advert but he didn't have anything for them to play. 'Could I notate music for string players?' I jumped at the chance – my first ever paid job for the grand sum of £100! I was over the moon. It's funny but I can trace my whole career back to that one job. I still work for that same producer, although now he pays me a little more!

My career has taken me on some fantastic journeys. As an orchestrator and arranger I've worked on films such as *Harry Potter* and with artists including Pavarotti, Melanie C and Simply Red. I think perhaps the highlight of my career so far was arranging the opening theme from *In The Night Garden* for a concert at the Royal Festival Hall performed by the London Philharmonic Orchestra. I also worked on every one of the episodes of the popular children's series *In The Night Garden* as a music editor and in 2009 wrote the music to a BBC One children's series called *Tronji*. There are ups and downs in any career, especially for people involved in the creative arts. However, I love the sense of achievement you feel after you've worked on a big project and see or hear the results on TV, cinema and radio. I enjoy the freedom my job brings and the excitement of not knowing what's around the corner. I have no idea what I'll be doing in ten years or even in 10 days but I hope I'm still making a living writing music.

I'm not sure I ever felt that North Parade was my home. Nowhere ever feels like the place you grew up; I left my home when I went to university and said goodbye to St Paul's Square. I enjoyed staying at North Parade, I spent long periods of time there in a lovely house on a great street, but it was very much Mum's home. When she was very ill in York Hospital I stayed there, sometimes with my brothers and aunt, occasionally by myself. It was a very difficult time for all of us. Now going back to York and in particular to North Parade involves facing a bewildering mix of feelings. There's a lot of sadness because I miss Mum and the times I spent in the house with her and my brothers.

After Mum died in 2008 it inevitably took a while to make a decision what to do with the house. Abi and I hadn't yet bought a property in London so after a lot of discussion it seemed the sensible thing for me to buy out my brothers' shares and take ownership with a view to renting it out. Its location makes it a good investment in what is a difficult time for the housing market. We were very fortunate that Abi knew a couple, Michael and Katie, who were looking for a place to rent. There's no doubt we all love York and North Yorkshire and make occasional trips back to the coast and the dales and York itself. Craig and Ross bring their young families. I toy with the idea of moving back to York, but this is not a practical option for any of us at the moment. I wonder if they, like me, would secretly like to return.

My overriding memory of North Parade is of Mum's happiness in her new house. I can still see the front door open so that neighbours can drop in, which they often did, the internal glazed door, shut but not locked, and Mum in the kitchen baking bread with Radio 4 playing.

*Postscript: March 30 2011:*
*Jim was conducting in the Albert Hall for a gala performance to celebrate Mikhail Gorbachev's 80th Birthday. He had done an arrangement for Melanie C, singer/songwriter and former Spice Girl, one of the performers in this special concert.*

Will

Tim

Jill

Jim in Abbey
Road Studios
Photo © Thomas
Bowles

Dorianne

Michael and Katie

Patrick and Karen

Megan and Gemma

Greg

Istvan and Monika

Raf

Millie, Mario and Rosalie

Libby, Dan and Josh

Janine

Party at Dorianne's to celebrate the Royal Wedding 29/04/2011.

# Dorianne
*Parrots and patchwork*

*Despite being plagued by arthritis there is still a fresh girlishness about Dorianne. The kitchen is a youthful blaze of colour with two huge fridge freezers, one orange, one lime green, and the place abounds with decorative parrots. They're even the motif on the scarf she is wearing.*

It was Jill who spotted the house for us; she'd been in this street for a couple of years. She was my dearest friend; we were young parents in Riccall, had shared the care of our boys who went to the same primary school, and had holidays together. We had such good times together. John and I are godparents to her youngest son.

I often say John was my destiny. We met in 1965. I was 18 on holiday in Devon. He was a maths student – had a summer job as a waiter. I spotted him – he spotted me. I still remember how he walked me back up the hill after we'd been out for an evening to the Chichester Arms. He was 20 that Friday and I bought him a packet of cigarettes. Suddenly at the station he asked for my address. His first visit to our family was memorable too: my brother Nick, a catering student, knowing John had been a waiter was showing off, balancing all the soup plates along his arm. They went everywhere, shattered on the hall floor! Because we had a special visitor, all was calm. John's verdict – mistakenly – was 'calm mother, calm daughter!' We were married in January 1967 in Alvaston, Derbyshire where my great-grandfather was a vicar. I'd been very embarrassed, mortified really, to discover our first son was already on the way – there was still such a stigma about things then – thought I shouldn't get married in a church, but Father said, 'Nonsense, of course you're having a white wedding.'

We spent the first three years of our marriage with John's parents in Rotherham where he was an articled clerk. Generations of their family had kept parrots; these Amazons with beautiful colouring were amazingly sociable creatures, sensitive to your moods. My sons had grown up with Josie – she was quite a character in our lives and came to visit us later when John's parents were on holiday. We were devastated when she died at 20. Her predecessor, Lizzie Peabody, had lived to be 130.

In 1972 we had moved to the village of Riccall outside York where John had become a manager at Creer, Etty, Rank, Chartered Accountants. We threw ourselves into village life, which for us revolved around St Mary's Church, the primary school PTA and the tennis club. I joined the Young Wives group and the Ladies Luncheon club. Over the years we hosted many parties there to raise money for good causes – it was great fun

It was a big thing moving here from Riccall, a community we'd been part of for nearly thirty years. But we had to think ahead. My hands were increasingly arthritic. It wasn't so easy to look after a big house and garden. The boys had left home and traffic on the A19 was getting worse by the year. So we decided to downsize and swap the commute for a ten-minute walk to work. This house had been divided into five bedsits for students, but at an earlier stage in its life it had been a shop. There was no central heating, the roof needed repairing, and we wanted to develop the loft. We finally moved in May 2000. It's a little oasis of peace once the school traffic is over. We've never regretted it and still keep in touch with our Riccall friends.

Home's been my domain really, though just sometimes I wish I'd followed a career path. I might have enjoyed being an interior designer. I trained in shorthand, typing and bookkeeping, at Miss Upton's Secretarial College in Leicester – very much old school – sit up and beg Old Imperial 66 typewriters. Heaven help you if you used a rubber! You had to do the whole thing over again. I'd found something I was good at. I became secretary to the principal of a coaching college in Leicester and worked till my first baby.

I started work again as a doctor's receptionist in Deighton near Escrick when my youngest was six. It fitted in well with the school run. Later I spent two years as the first paid secretarial assistant for St Leonard's Hospice which celebrates its 25th anniversary this year. I set up the support group in Riccall. I'm proud that it still goes strong. Now John is one of the Hospice's trustees.

In 1994 when the boys married, we opened our house for guests. We were in an ideal position on the main street between York and Selby. After my mother, who was widowed, came to Riccall in 1996 I had a helper. She often ironed sheets. She adored ironing! A perfectionist! She is currently recovering from a knee op. I know she's getting better – she's started telling me off!

*Some years ago Dorianne held an 80th birthday party at North Parade for her mum, Janine, a Belgian by birth, who was still fit enough to leap up onto a bench in the garden to thank her family for their treat of a hot air balloon flight. She spoke of her early involvement with the Belgian Resistance, cycling across Brussels with messages.*

Mother's stories of the occupation in Belgium would fill a book in themselves. At 18 she was a chocolate packer, a 'demoiselle vendeuse' in one of Brussels' most exclusive chocolate houses, Maison Sturbelle. She had to wear a little black dress with removable collar and cuffs and meticulously hand pleat the paper wrappers. She remembers one day when she was deliberately less meticulous than usual! A very large German walked in accompanied by a soldier and placed a large order. Janine realised she needed extra help and went into the back of the shop and told Madame that there was a 'Grosse Legume' (literally a fat vegetable – what we would call a Big Cheese) in the shop and that it was Goering. Madame laughed and said that couldn't be true. But it was indeed Goering with his baton in hand and other soldiers coming in and saluting him. What my mother and her young colleague Lousia delivered to the Hotel Metropole was not the usual precise quality box, but one in which they had carelessly crammed all the chocolates they didn't like. Every day for the next few weeks they lived in fear of arrest!

Mummy was so good at precision work and handicrafts I'd found it hard as a girl to live up to her. Then I learned patchwork. At last! I'd found something I could excel in. I've made quilts not only for her and my brothers, but all the young members of the family. The tally now is six grandchildren, three nephews, three nieces and four great-nephews.

Daddy met my mother on Christmas Eve 1944 when they were liberating Belgium. They married in July 1945 and came to live in Aylestone, Leicester with his mother who taught her English. I was born there in 1947 and have fond memories of this close-knit, extended family. My granny and her sister Dora, a headteacher, were neighbours in a horseshoe of semis with a shared orchard. Granny had been a teacher too, but in those days women had to stop teaching on marriage. With sons of my own I now understand more of what it would have meant for her to have her sons in the war.

Though suburban, it was an idyllic setting; such a safe environment. My two brothers and I were very companionable; I would often have to fit in with their games. I can remember playing cowboys and Indians, and how we used to run off across the road to play by the canal and in the fields without anyone worrying. Everyone had a little vegetable plot. I have a vivid memory of hollyhocks, nasturtiums and the hens my parents kept. So much of it is built up now. The school I went to had classes of forty in rows. Woe betide if you didn't do as you were told! We learned tables by heart, got our spellings right and read round the class.

Such a different world for our grandchildren. Our eldest son, David, a computer programmer, has a son and daughter who live quite close; Peter, an actuary – he calls that 'accountancy with fun' – lives over in Blackpool and has three girls and a boy, so quite a houseful when we're all together. We're often caught between wanting to support the young ones and having to deal with 'the elderlies'. I call it the sandwich generation. It was a distressing time when John's parents had to leave the house they'd been in for fifty years. Clearing a house is such a sad business and physically demanding too. It took thirty-three trips to the recycling depot to clear. His mother had had a stroke; his father, a well-loved doctor in Rotherham for four of those decades, died later in 2008. I was facing a second hip operation in the autumn. Jill had died that summer too. It seemed a particularly bleak time.

That year's big project was building an outhouse – a utility room, with ground-floor loo. We changed the kitchen door back to where it was 100 years ago, looking out onto the courtyard, now landscaped with raised beds. Come and have a look. Haven't the Christmas roses done well! So nice to sit out here if ever we get any sun! But above all it is practical. I'm trying to think ahead. I want to be able to stay in my own home for as long as possible, don't you? I keep busy: see Mum each week, volunteer at the Treasurer's House, do patchwork quilting and yoga and enjoy visits from the little ones.

John retires in 2011. I'm looking forward to it – I hope he is! He likes taking part in the Mystery Plays with the Scriveners Guild. He still enjoys cricket and the racing. We've had the loft fitted out so he will have his own special 'den'. But I'm also hoping we can scoot off on the Coastliner to Whitby for the day and enjoy some time together.

*Interview 10/03/10*

## Michael
*Alias Chief of the Weasels*

*I feel sure Jill would have loved her son's new tenants. Michael and Katie moved in across the road in January 2010. Michael proudly shows me the progress he's made with the garden, lots of new shrubs, a vegetable patch and a bird table.*

I don't suppose you know what this is sprouting under the cherry tree? *he asks. Mystery solved. It's lily of the valley, masses of it.*

We were renting a flat around the corner when we moved up from London – but to have a whole house to ourselves is just, well, we can't believe our luck. It's fantastic. I suppose I'm being a bit of a house husband at the moment. I've done bits of decorating too. It's good being here in York – great not to have to rely on the Tube; the scale of the place makes it much friendlier.

*Michael, a self-employed actor for nine years now, explains how in the acting world it's often also word of mouth that gets auditions through friends and agents. When he first moved here he was commuting to do Panto up at the Georgian Theatre in Richmond, and he's shortly to go into rehearsal for* Wind in the Willows *at the Theatre Royal in York where he will be Chief Weasel. I can imagine him enjoying that role, though he's not a bit weaselly in real life, either in stature or temperament – a tall, open, friendly character.*

It's a very special production; the whole theatre will be transformed.

*What drew him to this career? Was it a family thing?*

Oh no; not at all. I was more familiar with agriculture than acting. I was born in Cambridge but grew up in a very rural East Anglia – farm labouring stock going back six generations – way back to the 1750s, which is quite unusual. At first I thought this is very dull; but in a way I like that rootedness, being surrounded by evidence of family history, knowing when I pass The Green Man in Colne (Cambridgeshire) that the pub was run by my great, great-grandmother on her own at the turn of the century. I cycle past a huge flagpole in St Ives (Cambridgeshire) that commemorates the work of my great-granddad who remains the longest serving volunteer fireman in the area's history; he was station officer. I'm one of the few members of the family that doesn't live there still. As a kid I loved helping out on a local mushroom farm. Then I seem to remember early on I wanted to be a sports journalist. But I've always loved telling stories and entertaining.

There wasn't any sudden epiphany when I was at a play and said, 'Yes, that's for me!' Though I do have a very clear idea of the sort of theatre or way of working in theatre I like. I'm keen on the travelling player tradition and work that involves the audience and uses a lot of music. That's why I'm teaching myself the ukulele. [*There's a very dainty blue instrument on the kitchen table.*] I used to play the drums, but it's quite a bulky and inflexible thing on stage – then I moved to guitar. I reckon by the time I finish my career I'll be on the penny whistle or the triangle!'

To be honest, I think acting was the only thing I was any good at in school. I was always getting into trouble because of this booming voice I have; I find it impossible to whisper, got detentions even for loud mutterings. I always had to sit on my own at the back of the class; drama was the only place where my loud voice was an asset, where I could enjoy myself. I trained in Liverpool and moved down to London from there, thinking probably that's where all the action is, whereas in fact Liverpool is such a vibrant city, there's a lot going on in the arts there. Now I'm really keen to be part of this northern theatre scene.

*It must be difficult for actors when the work's not predictable?*

It's a bit like buses... you can sit around for three or four months then a couple of calls will come in quick succession. I read somewhere that the average actor works for seven weeks each year. I'm relieved to say I'm doing better than that, I've worked for over half the year… in the first six years I had winter and summer jobs – a good succession of work. At the moment I'm lucky to have been able to set up some teaching at the Theatre. York has the largest youth theatre in the country but there was no provision for adults so I'm doing some classes to raise skills with that group. Hang on a minute! [*Michael makes a dramatic exit – bounds out into the garden – I hear a vigorous 'shoo-shooing' and can imagine the flailing of arms as a cat is sent scampering away from his bird table.*]

*Did I hear you talk about winning an audition for work in South Africa?*

Oh, that was just an advert for a German yogurt filmed in SA with English actors. I didn't see much of South Africa; it's a very quick turnround, out one day, back the next – but fun. You really just don't know what's going to happen in this job, but you do know you're not going to be bored. There's no routine, no steady rising up the ranks or regular increments, but always the chance of a breakthrough to something special. An awful lot depends on luck, being in the right place at the right time. One example is the way a chance conversation in a Soho office gave me a part in a short film. It was called *Cashback*. It did really well and was nominated for an Oscar. In fact on my first date with Katie the waiter recognised me, asked me to sign a photograph; that's never happened before. Brilliant timing! *Not a set-up then! I tease.* Definitely not. *He and Katie have just announced their engagement.*

I met Katie in York when we were working on *Fungus the Bogeyman*, but it wasn't till later when we were in London that a romance began. So it's been good to move back here. All theatres have a digs list and Katie stayed at Hedley House Hotel when she was first in York, so we'd met Greg, who owns the house next door, back then. He did her a special rate for a long-term let. Katie's busy with three different productions on the go at the moment so you'll have to catch up with her later.

*And how's the latest member of the family settled in?* [*I'd been introduced to a muzzled greyhound from the animal rescue the previous week.*] It hasn't. We've had to take her back; we've never met such a troubled animal in our lives – couldn't cope. Come and see the replacement.

*In the corner of the front room is a neat, manageable aquarium.* Can you feed them on Saturday when I'm away? *No problem.*

*Interview 28/04/10*

*Postscript.* Wind in the Willows *was indeed a special production, made all the more exciting for my granddaughters by meeting Michael first and later discovering not only was he Chief Weasel, but also the horse pulling Toad's caravan, the judge sending him down and the barge woman helping him escape! Brilliant – the house is still resounding, 'Poop Poop!'*

## Katie

*The transforming magic of theatre*

My whole job is about transformation really. I start with these wonderful stories and translate them from the page to something dynamic. It's about making things accessible to a wider audience. I love the magic of it. How cool is that – to have a job with so much variety and the excitement of seeing all that happen. I feel so lucky to be doing this.

*Katie, a vivacious, energetic 30-year-old, is Associate Director of Pilot Theatre in York. She manages to fit this interview in between a workshop at the Theatre Royal and an interview with Radio Jersey. Meanwhile she asks, 'Do you like beans?' and presents me with a great armful of runners. The garden's clearly doing well. They'd just been sown when I interviewed Michael in the spring.*

*She co-directed* Wind in the Willows *with Damian Cruden of York's Theatre Royal. He knew he would have to be away to oversee the transfer of the spectacular production of* The Railway Children *to Waterloo station in London. I'd loved Mike Kenny's adaptation of these two children's classics.* The Railway Children *had two consecutive years' success at the National Railway Museum with a real steam train entering the auditorium at the end of each act. Both I and my grandchildren were enthralled.*

*Kenny's version of* Wind in the Willows *with its emphasis on old-fashioned virtues of friendship and neighbourliness and a special relationship with the natural world had a different sort of magic. I see Katie has a delightful print of Shepherd's illustration of Mole and Ratty on the river in their hallway.*

*When I went with my granddaughters Ella and Lucy to see the play we were sitting on the stage bank where the action normally is. As rabbits, hedgehogs and otters came past to enter the central arena they begged some sweets, much to the children's delight!*

It was a huge task to transform the main auditorium into a theatre in the round, but it's how everyone had envisioned it from the start and well worth it.

*Katie also co-directed* Romeo and Juliet — *an exuberant production with a lot of pace, energy and clarity. What's more it was visually stunning with the flower-strewn stage and the simple candle-lit framework backdrop. Katie and her co-director would be going out to see it safely installed in its various locations on tour from Aberystwyth to Edinburgh.*

*The third production she'd been involved with over the summer was an international project for an artistic network called Platform 11+ which brings together theatres from twelve European countries to collectively create new work for 11 to 15-year-olds. Their latest play was* The Mystery of Jack and the Clones of Chaos. *I see from her blog she's also been doing lots of workshops up and down the county.*

I always knew I wanted to do something creative. I couldn't bear the thought of doing a routine job. I suppose the interest in theatre started at school. I loved school and ran a drama club in the lunch hours. I was born in Paddington, then lived in Kenton but by the time I was 8 we were out in Pinner, a London suburb, just half an hour into the city. Early on I wanted to be an actress and followed my brother to uni. I studied Drama.

When I needed extra money I didn't do shop work. I did face-painting and box office work and later, after I left university, I did lots of workshops for schools and colleges. It was great getting an agent, my Equity card and first acting job, but I was aware of the need to earn *regular* money. I remember one project for Kingston Young Carers. I enjoyed that sort of work. I've produced educational resources for BTEC courses. The educational side of things is still important to me. This afternoon's workshop was about devised theatre.

But the change came when I decided to do a PGCE at Amersham. I needed to be qualified for a profession I could fall back on. I managed to arrange some teaching there two days a week while I studied. But by the third term they were asking me to do a full-time job. I was running the BTEC National Diploma course in Drama and Theatre Studies. There was an OFSTED inspection *and* I had a part in a play all at the same time. Manic.

I met Mark Hartly there and he asked me to direct all the BTEC and University shows. They went well and he was the one who kept saying to me, 'You're a director.'

In 2005 Mark set up his own production company; it was from him I got my first professional production, at 26. It was *The Government Inspector*, a fascinating play, but I had to do it with a cast of six instead of sixteen! A lot more work came my way. I wrote to Marcus Romer at Pilot Theatre who gave me a freelance job as Assistant Director on *Fungus the Bogeyman*. Michael was in that too. Even then when we were lodging in York he said, 'I could live here you know'. I thought that time would be a long way off, but we moved up a year and a half ago when I became Associate Director here.

I'm fascinated by the way Damian Cruden really knows his northern audience. He often suggests things I wouldn't have thought of – I'm just beginning to understand the differences in outlook. It's Takeover Month now when the Theatre is run by younger people. York Theatre Royal does an amazing amount of work with young people. I've been to a meeting this week with *Tutti Frutti*, based in Leeds, and *Belt Up* from York to share collaborative ideas about theatre. There's time now to pitch ideas, meet designers and writers, do more education work and plan for the next season. We will be doing a lot of ensemble work next year.

I've always loved London, but I am settling to life here, and we've made a lot of friends. Some neighbours from our last flat in St Olave's are coming for a meal tonight.

I'm Jewish and proud of my culture. I do keep some traditions. You might have noticed the mezuzah, the welcoming prayer fixed on the door. My mum is a very spiritual person, and what

I learned from her in my childhood was about different ways of loving people and loving the planet. Of course in York, as far as I can see there is no Jewish culture, no synagogue, no Jewish delis. And the awful history of Clifford's Tower (see footnote page 217). Mum just couldn't bring herself to go in.

But theatre is a powerful tool for understanding and exploring difficult areas of conflict. It can approach complex issues in a different way, help us shift our perspective and empathise with other people. I directed a couple of short plays in a trilogy about the Middle East. I felt very connected to these stories created by Naomi Wallace of real people's lives affected by the consequences and realities of war. I find theatre of this type exposes young people to different situations in a non-prejudiced way and allows them start conversations and form their own opinions about hugely complex situations.

Neither Mum nor Dad were directly involved with theatre, though they took a lot of interest in theatre and politics. David Hare's one of my favourites. My brother's gone down the political road. Mum is a children's party entertainer and Dad a wannabe Jewish comedian as well as being a chartered surveyor. My parents absolutely adore Michael; it doesn't worry them that he doesn't share their faith. I think I always knew when I grew up I would just want to marry someone I loved.

We complement each other well. I'm very ambitious to get on with things, to achieve; it's always 'must do this, must do that'. Michael's more relaxed. He calms me down, puts things in perspective and helps me appreciate what's already achieved so we can enjoy where we are now. As well as working hard we play hard, and we're currently planning our wedding for next May. There'll be a blessing by a Rabbi before a civil ceremony in South Cambridge. So there's a lot of exciting things in the air.

*It's time for Katie to rush home to speak to Radio Jersey about* Romeo and Juliet.

*Interview 12/10/10*

*Postscript: Spring 2011*

*Many arts organisations were fearing cuts to their funding in the new government's spending review. I noticed on the website of Pilot Theatre's artistic director, Marcus Romer, a comforting parable about a starfish which when mutilated simply grows more legs. York's Theatre Royal fortunately escaped.* The Railway Children *won a National Olivier prize for best entertainment and was about to be exported to Canada.*

## Will and the Golden Dalek
*On changing roles and role-play games*

*I'm not long into the interview before I realise that Will is an addict. He's totally hooked on RPG – live role-play games.*

Live role play is a bit like improvisational theatre. It's very exciting. I belong to a group in York. We meet in the home of one of the group members. One player becomes Games Master, sets a scenario and controls the overarching plot; each of the other players creates a character who can initiate sub-plots; together they develop situations and consequences. It's very absorbing. The story develops over several weeks, a bit like a TV serial drama with the first 'pilot' episode establishing the characters' backgrounds and what they are capable of.

*I hadn't known what to expect when I rang the door bell. Will was one of the few people to respond to my letter of whom I had no prior knowledge – not even a face to put to the name. The face turns out to be quite pale; it belongs to a slightly stocky man with dark hair, mid-thirties at a guess, with a quizzical expression behind the glasses. I introduce myself and light dawns on the face –* Oh, I'm so sorry! I'd forgotten it was tonight. *I offer to come back another day.* No, no, do come in. *An ironing board is hastily removed by a slim young woman with long hair who then disappears. Will insists he was the one doing the ironing as I'm led into a back sitting room/study. It reminds me somehow of the home of my childhood in the 50s – a comfy sofa, high bookcases, though these reveal an impressive collection of science fiction. A large golden Dalek is looking at me from the corner of the room.*

We work in all sorts of genres. At the moment I'm leading a gas lamp fantasy set in Bristol in 1835. It uses historic background but involves fantasy too. The players encounter the famous gunsmith Samuel Colt 'played' by the Games master, who really was in England at that time trying to find a manufacturer for his 'six-shooter' pistol. A few players can use magic – in this case mixing it with steam-powered technology, and fewer still possess God-given healing powers. RPG is very popular. There's a shop on Goodramgate that deals in games and comics you might have seen; it's called 'Travelling Man'.

*I'd never noticed this parallel universe before. I check its website; people using its forums have exotic logins and I wonder about Will; is he more likely to be a Kindredknight than a Hellsbelly? One group needs a new player – they've lost one to a Guppy's club group: We meet on alternate Thursdays. Not into hack and slash or dungeons. (Phew!)*

*There are other invitations:*

'Pop in and get your fill of new comics. Looks like the sacrifice to the Volcano god worked! – Come to a signing day for *The Walking Dead* by Charlie Adlard.'

*Zombies apparently will walk in Leeds on April 17th.*

'Buy now! Post-apocalyptic Times, 2029 Online – a skill-based epic sci-fi MMORPG rich in landscapes and player experiences. Participate in cooperative quests, player-killer matches and special skirmishes.'

*How did Will become an RPG fan?*

A teacher got me interested to encourage my writing and maths skills.

I grew up in Rochester, Kent. My parents built their own house; we could see the river, and the fields beyond the garden went down to the water. Of course, there was a power station dominating the skyline. Dad had trained as a chef, and still loves cooking, as I do, but he hated spending his days in hotel basement kitchens; he'd arrive before dawn, go away after dusk. Six months of not seeing the sun was enough. He became a fireman, but hurt his back and was invalided out just six months before he would have received his twenty-year medal. That still upsets him. He drives coaches now. Mum, initially an industrial chemist, retrained as a teacher and still works part time.

I thought of it as a fairly conventional childhood, but I did spend a lot of time in boats – we went to Holland each year for a few weeks. Dad's been there so often he's now a paid-up member of a yacht club over there. I was in Rochester till I was 18. I have two brothers, both now separated; one has recently gone back to live with my parents; they've downsized now. The other, who has two children, is living on a boat there.

As for beliefs, environmental issues are important to me so I tend to vote liberal. I was brought up a Catholic, but now veer towards Buddhism, more the creationist side of things. Some entity must have set all this going.

Trish, my other half, grew up in Carlisle. We met as undergraduates at Bradford. I was doing Technology and Management. I'd tried Chemistry – that didn't work out so I was having to self-finance my studies. I took a year's sabbatical to get some money together.

We've just announced a date for our wedding in October. It's only been a fourteen-year engagement! We've had lots of congratulations from friends on Facebook. I must say I don't find letter writing or phone conversations easy. Facebook suits me because you can build up a dialogue over a few days. Trish prefers to blog and has an iPhone. She's busy upstairs on the computer now.

After we'd graduated and worked a while we had three months travelling; flew to San Fransisco – had rail passes; travelled to New Mexico, saw Hot Springs, renamed Truth or Consequences after the quiz show in 1950! Las Vegas was just surreal. On then to Texas – then to Florida – went due south to Key West – saw Ernest Hemingway's house. Did you know they have six-toed cats there? Then up the east coast as far as Lake Placid. Finally Route 66 all the way back to San Francisco by Greyhound. Then, oh dear, back to normal working life.

I don't feel I'm yet in a job I want to do for life. When I first came to York I worked for Jarvis Rail. I was the last to be recruited before the damning report into the Hatfield crash was published, so I was the first to be made redundant when they lost contracts then.

*David Hare's play,* The Permanent Way, *premiered in York in 2003, explored both the consequences and wider causes of that and the subsequent Potter's Bar rail disaster. Hare used material from the transcripts of the investigation, which highlighted shortcomings with the track maintenance. Network Rail say this is all done in-house now. Plans for track renewals have been cut back as the recession bites. Jarvis were about to go into administration as we spoke, leaving 2,000 Jarvis employees in York at risk.*

I've had a few changes of role since then; I worked for Norwich Union (Aviva) in insurance, but did I really want this to be my career? I tried to do a Masters in teaching but that didn't work out. I'm back with Aviva now doing IT support. They too of course have been cutting back. I don't think my own job is in danger, but it's not a good situation. I'm really looking for something that offers new challenges and gives some job satisfaction.

I've been writing short stories, science fiction mostly, targeting the American market, but no success yet.

*I ask if he's joined any of York's many writing groups but it sounds as if he prefers to work on his own. The bookcases are packed with sci-fi books. They both love reading. Will is a Terry Pratchett fan and likes Lois McMaster Bujold. He particularly recommends her* Ethan of Athos *in which advanced technology makes possible an all male society. The plot involves interplanetary espionage, genetics, and newts!*

That's Trish's special bookcase over there. The photos are of her nephews, and her father who died last year of cancer. It took hold so quickly.

Trish, who studied Environmental Science, is a transport planner with the council now. She's had a bit to do with York's plans for Cycle City. [*York was awarded Cycling City status and £3.68m of government money to improve facilities and get more people cycling.*] One of their better initiatives.

*I noticed pink pennants flying from York's lampposts advertising a Fun Cycle Week in July. Trish will be one of many council employees moving by 2012 into a new Civic Headquarters building at Station Rise. There was a huge consultation exercise before they opted to regenerate this historic building in the city centre. There has been a lot of work on public buildings this year; the Central Library and the Yorkshire Museum closed this spring for major refurbishment, completed before the current round of funding cutbacks.*

The cutbacks are already being felt by the planners; they are having to rethink their plans.

We've been in York about eight years. We like walking around the city, love the atmosphere; we enjoy things like the Open Air Shakespeare Project, and stopping in at Yorkshire Brewery pubs! We moved to this rented house five years ago from a flat near Monk Bar thinking we'd spend a couple of years collecting furniture and save for a deposit. I've enjoyed having a bit of garden here. At the point when house prices dipped, banks weren't lending mortgages, so here we still are. We like this area, but very much doubt we'll be able to afford our own house here.

Incidentally, the Dalek, which is remote-controlled, belongs to Trish. But she has taken a step back from role-play games – finds it too obsessive.

*I wonder what the Dalek makes of this and wish them well for the future.*

*Interview 17/03/2010*

*Postscript:*
*Will and Trish were married in October and moved to a new home in January 2011.*

# Tim and the Chien Lunatique

*There's a warning at the door: Chien Lunatique. I know the dog in question – it glories in the name of Haggis. It's dark-haired and dark eyed and, dare I say, dark-tempered? Soulful perhaps. Its owner, Tim, is blond, blue-eyed and extremely good-humoured. He tells me his family have always had Cairns and at 9 the dog is less lunatic than he was. Well, apart for the odd shirt-eating episodes – and funnily it's often Ian's shirts he goes for, rather than mine. They don't really get on. I'd met Ian, Tim's partner a few years earlier, but knew Tim several years before he became a neighbour and a colleague at York St John; we have a couple of mutual friends whom he'd met as a student in Ripon from 1983-7.*

I always liked the atmosphere of York – knew I wanted to work there but left it late finding my first teaching job; one turned up at Cawood. It was a small traditional C of E village school. I remember when I first started it still had one of those three-figure telephone numbers! The interview was in the vicar's dining room out at the vicarage in Cawood; it felt like something out of *Cider With Rosie*. The children would bring you presents of things like rabbits that needed gutting! Then I was in Harrogate for six years before I got a Deputy Headship at St Barnabas across the river in York. You still had to do classroom work as well as admin and be good at both. When the Head came back from maternity leave after I'd been Acting Head I felt it was time to move on – roles had rather got messed up then. That's when I got the job at York St John.

*You'd find a big change moving into H.E.?*

Oh, yes, a massive change. I remember my first lecture, we're talking about 2000. I told them to go into groups to do things

– and they did it – no problems; got to 11 o'clock and no wet pants to deal with. Brilliant! It's really refreshing working with young people. I feel really privileged to be going out into lots of different situations, working with different local authorities. There's a massive amount of flexibility, but the rhythm of the school year isn't the same as in primary. You can get totally unpredictable huge workloads at times of year when you would have been on holiday before. My main responsibility is for the part-time programme, the Post Graduate Certificate of Education. There are lots of mature students embarking on career changes. They bring a lot of their previous experience to the course, which is great. I really like teaching them.

I moved here from St Mary's two streets back. I'd lived there for twelve years; it had a bit of a London feel to it. A lovely community. There were a couple of people across the road who were artists; their house was the hub of the street where friends would gather for a chat in the evenings – really nice. I bought the flat from a country landowner who'd purchased the whole block and was selling off one at a time to fund his retirement. I knew about this street here, liked it, saw it as an interesting sort of backwater. Initially I was interested in your house.

*Martyn my solicitor, another mutual friend, hadn't let on. Tim, a very keen cook, would have been drawn to the Aga; he installed a larger one in the house he eventually bought; his kitchen looks out onto a leafy yard, filled mostly with a large lilac tree.*

I couldn't sell the flat. Eventually I decided I could hold on to it and rent it out and bought this with a bit of help from my parents. When I did come to sell the flat ten years later, prices had soared and that's when I bought my place in France.

*I've called in on Tim when I've been in France staying with Chris and Jo, our friends who have a place nearby; it was through them he got to know the area. Kath, Kildip and Daniel have also stayed at his house. It's perched on a hill overlooking a sleepy village in the Aveyron which has a lovely duck pond and a little auberge, Chez Mimi, famed for its great Sunday lunches.*

*How's it going out there?*

I love it. It's actually got nicer over the years. I know more people there now; the couple I bought the house from are lovely and live down the road and there are some other neighbours who have been doing up the property next door at La Tour. Their house was basically a ruin when I moved in. His son came to stay here with me in York for a couple of months. He eventually got a house for the year and a job at the Spurriergate Centre as a waiter.

It felt at home moving here as I already knew Kath across the road through a mutual friend, a chaplain – another Lancastrian living in York. She had these street barbecues which helped me get to know people. That's how I met Daniel and Kildip.

*But your house is for sale now?*

Yes, I'm moving to Scarborough. Ian and I committed to a civil partnership some years ago but mostly because of work kept our separate houses. It was funny, when we went to Langtoft where Ian lives to have the banns called – it's between Driffield and Scarborough where he teaches French – they said, 'Oh, we've never done one of those before,' and they had to draft in someone from Bridlington to supervise. The banns were eventually published at Driffield.

We'd met in York and found we'd got a lot of things in common; both our families come from strong Methodist roots; we found we knew the same obscure hymn tunes! We both came from Lancashire – Ian's from Preston – we both love music, both teach, both love France. 'Coming out' to our families took a long time for us to deal with. We lived at a distance from them and didn't declare everything that was going on… had friendships that might have indicated other lives… but a time comes when enough is enough… you have to be true to yourself… stop pretending. As you get older it's easier to be confident with who you are. Working at York St John was also an extremely liberating experience too as opposed to working in a school situation. They were very supportive of individuals in all their differences. I feel that it would have been much harder if I'd still been working in a local primary school. I was lucky that I was able to introduce Ian to my parents first as a friend; they got to know him as a person, really liked him, so while they weren't wild about the civil partnership, they supported me because they could see we were good together, that it was right for me.

So we've been splitting the week between the two homes. I've come to the decision that Scarborough with Ian is much better than York on my own. I feel I can make that move now. I've gradually made some good friends over there and got involved with his ecumenical choir. It's the right time now. My work is more flexible, so I'll be the one doing the commuting. I'll make sure I take my research time too.

*Weren't you doing a comparative study about the Swedish education system?*

Yes, I did that for my doctoral thesis. I've always been interested in international education, but, you know, it was our friend Chris who started that link. In our last year at college she was responsible for putting on entertainments for the visiting Swedish students, invited me along; that's when I met my Swedish friend Larz. He and I kept in touch. Later I helped organise work experience for his students in health care through my friend Clare who works at the hospital. It's her allotment that Sue and Janette share.

I set up some projects that fed into my research. I was intrigued that children out there didn't have the early demands which resulted in a sense of failure and labelling that our children have here. Over here children had to be seen doing things; over there they were allowed to be out in the open just sitting and thinking. Ten Swedish institutions and ten English ones had to take photographs of what they perceived to be a typical day, which involved sorting activities they thought significant in their learning. The Swedish photographs included pictures of children sitting round a table for meals with the staff and with a cloth on and candles lit. It was clear to them that talking, socialising and reflecting were learning experiences. There was no equivalent in the English photos.

*Our friends Chris and Joe were coming round to my house for supper that night. Tim was glad to join us. They greeted him warmly, enquired about the house move: 'And what's the fall-back plan if Ian and Haggis can't cope in one house?' Chris asks. 'He won't have to go back to your mum and dad in Standish, will he?'*

Well I hope we find a way to make it work; dog walking amenities were part of the criteria when we chose the house. It's certainly added to my pleasure here, getting to know other dog owners in the street on walks by the river.

*Standish is on the outskirts of Wigan and I remember with embarrassment how I'd first discovered Tim's Lancastrian origins. Many years ago Tim was asking about my daughter's hunt for her first job. 'Oh she seems to have found a good job, it's for a big American carpet company – but it's in Wigan of all places,' I said, in a tone that implied Timbuktu would be preferable. Tim laughed. Once I'd discovered and apologised for my gaffe Tim gave me some contact numbers for her; friends of his were moving out of a good rented house that might be of interest to her. She followed it up and they took to each other so well she went with them to fill the empty room in their new place. So thanks to Tim she had a good start in Wigan, 'of all places'.*

*'Hope the sale's going through, we're booked in to stay with you for Scarborough Jazz Festival later this year,' Chris reminded him before they left.*

*Interview 21/06/2010*

## Karen
*On being your own boss*
## Patrick
*On being a physio*
## Together
*On being a family*

*It's election day when I finally get chance to talk to Karen and Patrick. They lead very busy lives. It's the end of a working day, when they're probably both shattered. I remember that feeling of just wanting to come in and slump all too well. But I'm touched to see them holding hands while we talk.*

**K:** Patrick and I probably first met ten years ago. But it was only after Tim (a good friend from my student days) invited us both for dinner in 2004 that we first got together. At that time I was living not far away in a brand new flat in Grosvenor Terrace. Before that I had lived and worked in Boston Spa. Patrick took the girls to school in Boston – we must have passed each other loads of times before we really knew each other. I owned a rambling old town house there. It certainly had character; it dated back to about 1814. I'd enjoyed moving to a new place in York where everything worked! My flat, though large, wasn't suitable as a family home. Patrick, who had a house to sell at Church Fenton at that time, had wanted to live in this area too, so we began house hunting.

Again it was when we were visiting Tim that we noticed this house for sale. Patrick had always liked this street. I wasn't keen because of the parking! But I like the area and the house. There was enough room for the girls here too, though the attic conversion this year has made a big difference for them. We've gradually been sorting the house together to suit our own needs and tastes. We were married from here, it must be nearly three years ago now, at the Grange followed by a blessing at Byland Abbey. A lovely day.

What matters most to all of us at the moment is building a strong family home. Until I met Patrick, I'd always lived in my own space; though there was a lot of family around when I was young. I was born in Halifax and brought up in Elland. Mum was the middle one of ten and I have a sister with seven children. There were huge adjustments to make here at first, for everyone, but the girls are great, very lively, there's a lot of laughter.

**P:** I travelled a lot as a child as my father was in the army. I was born in Germany. We lived in Chatham briefly, then Australia for a year and a half, then Ripon (long before the place was significant in Karen's life), then had quite a long time in Malta. I'd be 10 when Dad came out of the army and settled in New Malden, but as a civil engineer he still spent a lot of his time abroad. Mum was busy at that time with her German father, helping her mother at their home in Germany to care for him. A lot of my time as a youngster was measured out with rugby and cricket training sessions and matches. I'd always been keen on sport and became interested in physiotherapy so arranged several weeks of work experience at a variety of hospitals. I went on to study in London, one of the few places offering a degree course in that subject then.

**K:** I started working life in a temporary job in a brewery! But I run my own business now. I was first responsible for developing links between schools and industry when I worked for the Industrial Society in Leeds. Then I had several years working first as an account manager and eventually as a director for a publishing business at Thorp Arch and Boston Spa. It was a good job in many ways, but it was a bit frustrating in that I was the only non-family member on the board of this small company.

While I was there I studied part time for the MBA (around 1993 so quite a while ago). Though I have to say there was so much reading to do that I've not got back into the habit of reading for pleasure since. I used to read a lot. I'd studied French and English Literature for my first degree at Ripon College. That's where I met Tim; we've been friends ever since so it's been good to have him as a neighbour.

It would be 2000 when I decided to leave to set up my own business. This enterprise involves cooperation with many different freelancers and web-designers, as well as working with teachers, children and education advisors to produce educational resources.

My premises are out at the Science Park – they have great facilities there, but I have to travel widely to meet with clients and clarify the exact brief and target audiences for the projects. Every one of them is different so there's no boredom. For example, I worked with Manchester Airport to produce a teaching resource pack for use with 4-year-olds. It provided information, posters and curriculum ideas and activities which enabled teachers to turn the classroom space into an airport. This helps create the sense of a real context in which to do role play and develop language, literacy and numeracy and life skills. By contrast, another more recent project was producing a website for Betty's cookery school.

Being your own boss has its advantages, but being responsible for generating all of the income and managing cash flow can be stressful. I often work long hours. It's hard to switch off sometimes when it's your own business. It makes it hard to plan ahead for holidays. Doesn't it?

*Karen gets a sympathetic nod of agreement from Patrick.*

**P:** My work as a physio involves much more regular hours, a daily commute to Pontefract and a lot of hard physical work as well as paperwork. I see a lot of patients with low back pain or chronic neck pain. A great deal of the work is about self-management of the patients' symptoms. Chronic pain seems to be on the increase.

*I ask about what I perceive to be a huge shortage of physiotherapists in hospitals. He explains a lack of a joined-up policy.*

A government pledge was made to fill the gaps so extra training places were created. Exactly at the point when more physios were graduating than ever before, hospitals started cutting back on provision because of the financial squeeze. There are probably plenty of unemployed physios about. The problem is doctors and nurses have a much higher public profile than physiotherapists; there is limited understanding of how we contribute to healthcare. Further cuts could well fall on our departments, but I don't know where. I'm working at a fairly senior grade now, we all have big workloads.

**K:** We're about to go and vote, but I suspect, regardless of the outcome of the election, the national deficit means cutbacks are inevitable, so firms might look at the sorts of educational services I offer as dispensable.

At home it's simple things we love – just sitting round on a Sunday morning and reading the papers together and chatting about them. Gem's been interested for a while and now Meg takes a real interest and has quite a lot to say too. They were particularly interested when Barack Obama was elected America's first black president last year.

**P:** We enjoy playing tennis with them and go off for days out. Fountains Abbey is a favourite spot, but we love the coast too; Runswick Bay, Filey. We can chat while we're walking. And of course there's the dog to walk. Sadly one of our two rescue dogs died recently. We love the walk along the river bank from here towards the Ings at Clifton. We seem to spend a lot more time talking about getting fit rather than doing anything. We do both love skiing though and we've just had a skiing holiday on our own.

**K:** I look forward to holidays you know, but when I come back, it's funny, it feels so good to come home to York. I feel really glad we live here.

*Interview 06/05/2010*

## Sisters Meg and Gem (16 & 14)

*Half-term break, homes, homework and how others see us*

*I'd spoken to Meg and Gem, the girls next door, earlier in the year. It was their half-term. Patrick, their dad, had shown me in. Karen was away at East Midlands Airport, one of many client groups for whom she produces educational material. 'Something about their impact on the environment,' she'd explained. The girls are keen to be part of my project, but first I must go up to see Meg's new attic bedroom. Her move means that her younger sister Gem can now upgrade from the smallest room in the house to the middle bedroom which is currently standing empty – about to get a facelift.*

*The loft space was being converted just before Christmas, a longer job than anticipated as the builder – the same guy who did my bathroom last year and Jill's the year before – was laid low by the swine flu virus. It's looking great and Meg, clearly well pleased with it, sits cross-legged on her bed in the centre of this bright, light space, all freshly painted and carpeted. Over in one corner a pile of much-loved soft toys look equally pleased with their new home; a dreamcatcher sparkles at one of the windows; to one side is a desk and computer. Patrick tells me,* 'Karen and I came up here on New Year's Eve – had a great view of all the fireworks!'

*The two girls will be the youngest in this collection of stories. Do you remember where you were at the Millennium? You'd have been just 6 and 4 then?*

**G:** Yes I do! We were at the Village Hall in Boston Spa – I remember a massive net of balloons that was let down at midnight.

*Their time is divided between here and their other home, in Bilbrough at their mum's. I don't know the place. Is Tadcaster the nearest town?*

156

**M:** There's just one main street; a butcher and a small supermarket, that's about it.

**G:** Well, don't forget the florist! It's good being so near York's shops here. Especially at Christmas.

*Do you see this as home?*

**M and G:** Definitely.

**G:** We've got a good set-up here. Some of our friends aren't so lucky. Some have no contact with one parent at all.

**M:** Wouldn't even want to see their other parent.

*They seem happy and well-adjusted. Is it a logistical problem with two homes?*

**M:** Clothes can be a problem. Gem's better at organising things than me.

**G:** Well, some things. We both enjoy riding and of course the horses Heidi and Ben stay at a farm near Bilbrough. I rode out this morning. I can't do that on a school day. There's a lot of work involved, mucking out daily, getting Heidi in on winter evenings. We once had a special riding holiday in Romania. It was so beautiful. Do you remember when we saw fields being ploughed with oxen?

**M:** Yes, and those lovely old-fashioned haystacks all gathered round a big branch.

*I recall my own amazement on my first visit to Timisoara in 1999, a Socrates teaching exchange, seeing old ways of life coexisting with the new.*

*If there's a concern about youngsters not exercising enough it doesn't apply to them. The girls are both very energetic, though Meg confesses,* 'I'm not a morning person!'

**G:** I swim Fridays and Sundays. Megan is a tennis player. She's doing really well!

**M:** I'm the youngest of the Copmanthorpe Ladies team.

*I ask about role models.*

**G:** I admire athletes, the tremendous discipline they have to achieve success.

*The girls are very well travelled; they have been lucky enough to have had lots of skiing holidays in France, spent a lot of childhood holidays in Turkey, have been to Crete and Germany. Meg says she'd love to travel to Africa. They've been watching the TV series about the Rift Valley, but also heard about Africa from Karen's brother.*
*What are they going to be doing at half-term?*

**M:** Well I was 16 yesterday! I bought my first lottery ticket. Karen's niece is coming over this afternoon. Later this week I'm going on a special celebration outing to London with a friend.

**G:** There'll be coursework to fit in as well. It's my first year of GCSE year and I'm wishing now I'd chosen at least one creative option, I'm finding it a bit tedious.

**M:** I've already had to state my options for 'A' level. I've chosen Chemistry, Biology, History and French. Some will be doing five subjects. Medicine might be a career choice – Dad's a physiotherapist and Mum's a doctor; or I like the idea of Law, or even veterinary practice.

**G:** I'm not sure yet. But definitely a career. We're treated just the same as the boys. Same expectations of everyone. Same chances.

*They've been encouraged to socialise from an early age, know adults in a wide range of work situations 'and some with no work!' A report out this year said British children are the most examined and stressed in Europe. Gem escaped year 9 SATS as a result of this. I expect they'll look for sympathy, but far from it.*

**G:** Well I think assessment is a good thing. At least you know where you are.

**M:** And it gives you targets. And prepares you for what's coming.

*So do you have a system for fitting in all this study?*

**G:** Well, mostly Sunday nights!

*They're concerned that a lot of older people have images of gangs of threatening 'hoodies' when they think of their age group.*

**M:** I suppose there are gangs, even at Tadcaster, but they're a small minority. Though we do know quite a lot of kids who drink and smoke and do drugs. I sometimes think the kids' parents are complicit in this.

**G:** It's shocking how easily accessible drugs are. Anything you wanted you could get.

*How effective are anti-drug advertising campaigns and education at school?*

**G:** It's hopeless; they just dance round the subject. They never get to the point.

**M:** It is a bit of a worry for the future when so many of my generation are so messed up.

*And what about your hopes, Meg?*

**M:** Well it would be wonderful if they could find out more about the universe; things that are still a mystery now.

*Interview 16/02/2010*

*Postscript: Megan achieves fantastic results from her GCSE year. She moves to Bootham School in September. I get an invite to their Thursday lunchtime concert series.*

## Greg
*Student, landlord, hotelier, tsunami survivor*

*Greg was a student himself when he lived in the house opposite. He now rents it out and also owns Hedley House Hotel in nearby Bootham Terrace. He and his young family are currently living at Shipton village. He's babysitting on the evening of the interview and his friend Mark is with him.*

The house in North Parade belonged to my dad. He'd previously used it for holiday lets but when I started studying at Askham Bryan I shared it for three years with some of my mates, including Mark here. I didn't have to pay rent because I did the caretaker bit.

Do you remember that police raid? There was a fire in the bins in the back garden. Aerosols were popping. Someone thought it was a great idea and went and collected all the aerosols in the house and put them on. The field at the back of the house was ablaze. It was like something out of a war film. Police came across with dogs like an armed response team. I think they thought we'd got a bomb factory.

I own it now; most of my good friends have lived there in the past. And some professional working couples. Now I use it for staff accommodation for the hotel, *Hedley House*. They come from all over; we've had South Africans, Australians, Scots, Thais, and there was a Greek guy. He was a right muppet.

*Why so many overseas people?*

They're the ones that apply. It's seasonal too. I've interviewed a Polish lad today – he was good; he'd travelled a bit. They have a bit more about them when they've travelled. I went round the world for a bit myself; the agricultural engineering stuff helped me get jobs on the way. There's a young Hungarian couple in there now who'd be happy to be in the book.

I was just 8 when we first moved to York. My parents had sold their house in Barking and bought these two derelict houses in Bootham Terrace. People thought they were mad. It was minging. Piles of mouldy cat poo everywhere. We moved from floor to floor around the builders. They were turning them into a hotel. It was great! Mum has the vision, the foresight, the ideas. Dad provides the money. Hedley House opened in 1984. I own that as well now. I bought it off me dad ten years ago. We've just been shortlisted for York's Hotel of the Year Award.

I love renovating properties. I've done a few now. We've just done up number 20. Everything was ripped out – only the roof and the walls left. The floors were rotten. It's OK when you know your builders. We dropped the ceilings to get a loft conversion. Six bedrooms – five ensuite – and a kitchen. It's self-catering holiday lets. It's up and running now.

I love York, there are so few of the typical city problems here, but what have we got left apart from the tourist industry? No Terry's, no sugar beet, no Ben Jonson, no railway workings. The industry's leached out of the place. I'm a bit worried about competition from the development of the Terry's site. There seem to be lots of new hotels going up.

I moved out to the village here three and a half years ago. It was hard. That hotel was my baby. In fact you've given me an idea. I'm going to start a yearbook about the hotel. There've been lots of stories there. But we were starting a family. I put a manager in. She's Lithuanian. She's good. And my wife, Lou, works with me now. We work well together. She'd been a PE and maths teacher before; she started at Knottingly, then she got this bad school with lots of problems and I said, 'work for me till you find something better,' and she's never looked back. She's away this week so I'm minding the kids. She sees to it that I make an effort with them. I don't leave home till about 9.30 and I'm generally back for them at 4. [*There are toy tractors about and a baby monitor.*] We've been skiing with them. The eldest, Harrison, he's 4 now; he can do a red run without crashing!

I find time to keep fit; I go to the gym, run, shoot things. *Shoot things?* Well, pheasants. *'And don't mention the darts,' his friend chips in.* No we're rubbish. We've only played six times – it's the pub on a Tuesday night. It's good fun, though.

Lou and me had only been together a year and a half before we were married, though we'd actually met on a skiing holiday when we were 15. We were quite sure we wanted to marry. We were on honeymoon on Koh Phi Phi on Boxing Day, 2004 when the tsunami struck. We'd been away for about ten days by then, had come over to this island to join some friends. For a few hours I thought I'd lost her. I've written about it. You're the first person to see it. I wrote it for myself. First thing I've ever written since school.

### Koh Phi Phi, Boxing Day, 2004

I felt water rushing in by my ankles, looked back to see Lou, her face all confusion and fear. Behind her – a mountain of black water – people screaming – the rumble of the wave getting closer. In a split second I was underwater. What the hell is going on! I didn't read this in any guide book!

The water was a thick stinking slug of sand, glass, metal and wood so powerful, so, so powerful. It spun me around, tearing the clothes from my body. I felt my T-shirt rise up, lifted my arms so it did not hinder me in any way. Debris was battering me from all sides. This could kill me, I thought, blocking my face and chest with my arms, pushing the big lumps away as best I could. Still in complete disbelief, I thought of Lou – prayed she would be OK. I didn't know which way was up.

Then I popped up from the filthy water and gulped a lung full of air. I was in a dark room, the water still charging along. I could see a window coming up; knew I had to get through it; knew if I got stuck I would die. The water was rising quickly; I was near the ceiling; I brought my legs up to my chest and prepared to try and kick the window out. Thankfully the debris smashed the window for me. I surfaced next to the sloping roof of another property. The water was rushing around the corner in front of me down a narrow alley. I didn't want to go round that corner as I couldn't see what was there. If I got trapped in a pile of debris – that would be it.

I clung to the roof but the tiles had no ridges to get my fingers around, so I pressed my arms flat trying to use the surface area of my skin to help me 'stick' to the roof. Water was still rushing round the corner trying to drag me away. I put my arm into the building under the water. I could feel a rolled up blind which made a better anchor, but half expected it to come away. Finally the water started to ebb. Back on the ground I found a sarong to cover my now naked body. It was silent apart from an odd whimper. I went back into the building looking for Lou. The floor of brown muddy puddles was littered with debris; it was surreal moving through the devastation.

Would more building come crashing down? Were there any live electricity cables? As I stood looking for the best way through, I realised I was on a smashed window frame; jagged edges of glass surrounded my bare feet, but I felt no pain! I saw some movement. Two men were trapped in the debris. One, a Scandinavian, was upright but with his arms and legs twisted, completely dazed and bewildered. I had to get him out first to reach a Thai, who did not speak English. I pulled him out bit by bit, nodding after each pull to make sure he was OK.

My worry was Lou. *She is a strong girl, if I have survived she will have*, I kept telling myself. *But if she was trapped, she might die if more water comes.* I looked and looked. But no Lou.

In the next building, lying half on a precariously balanced mattress was a naked Scandinavian lady, white as a ghost, screaming for help; her leg was cut in half from her knee to her ankle. The room was trashed; I had to climb over all sorts of debris to get to her. Trying to stay calm, I made her as comfortable as possible, tore a sheet that was nearby, folded her leg back together and wrapped the sheet around her leg. I could not move her on my own; even if I could where would I take her? I felt awful leaving her, but I had to find Lou.

People were starting to panic again and I wanted to get higher. I struggled to reach the roof of the next building. A number of people there had gathered in silence looking around. One saw his wife and a daughter on a building in the distance, but he was missing another daughter. One lady could see her husband. The young Swedish lads had lost a friend. They were kind enough to get me some clothes but I still needed to look for some trainers or flip-flops. The flooded buildings were eerily silent and stinking of sewage. It felt wrong going into people's rooms. No luck!

From the back of this building to the next I leapt a two-metre gap. It was like being a kid again! I had to walk along some tin ridge tiles and burnt my feet in the process. I came face to face with Alana – we had spent the previous day on a boat trip. 'Have you seen Gary?' she asked. 'No. Have you seen Lou?' 'No.' She looked battered and had a cut leg.

I teamed up with another English lad to look for people. We could hear a muffled cough and he could see something. 'There!' He'd reached an unconscious girl, about 13 or 14 years old. She was a dead lump and difficult to move. The puddles near her were deep – I am surprised neither of us got hurt lifting her out. I put her on a bed in the recovery position and got someone to watch her. I was now starting to really worry about Lou. PLEASE GOD, PLEASE!

The next man I came across was in a really bad way. A tarpaulin had been swept away, collected lots of debris, hit a coconut tree and bent a piece of scaffolding around it trapping the man by the head. He was screaming a bloodcurdling scream. Three or four uninjured guys were painstakingly trying to free him. I felt I was in the way and headed back, calling out for Lou as I walked.

Two and a half hours had passed. I could feel myself flagging, drained of energy. Alana was where I had first seen her with a small group of people. As I approached she asked me again. Her look was still of total despair. 'No – sorry!' Then from somewhere behind her my name was being called! 'Yes, yes here,' I yelled out. A German guy had come from the next hotel. 'Lou is in our room, she is injured but OK.' She was alive. I started to shake. THANK YOU GOD!

In the foyer there were about twelve bodies, lifeless and bloated. Some had doors to cover them; on one was a roughly picked bunch of flowers. As we climbed the stairs we passed the receptionist who recognised me, smiled and touched my arm. 'Lou's quite badly hurt.'

I prepared myself for the worst. I was just thankful she was alive. I walked into the room and Lou's face lit up. I rushed over and carefully hugged her.

*The last line is a relief… but also worrying?*

Yes, she survived – she had a nasty cut in her chin, a black eye but nothing worse. I only had superficial cuts, damaged ribs, my feet were bad, but in that environment cuts went sceptic and I was in a wheelchair for a bit.

Yes, it changed me completely. Right from the day after. It brings home what matters. I think it was good for me in a weird way.

*He shows me before and after pictures on his laptop.*

This is where we were standing; that was the beach; that was the hotel; you can see how high the debris is piled, how much it's changed the contour of that coastline. Our friends survived too. We've just been to see them in Canada. She's expecting her third child at the moment. We're lucky. 230,000 died in the tsunami.

*Interview 24/02/2010*

## Istvan and Monika: Greg's Hungarian tenants

*A plasterer and his bible; a housekeeper at Hedley House*

We grew up in Bonyhád, a small city of about 14,000 people in the Tolna county of southern Hungary close to the Danube. An attractive city. The river is just a couple of miles away. There are lots of trees, interesting architecture, beautiful churches. It's a Catholic community; my grandmother is very religious but most people my age are no longer actively interested in the Church. Monika and I met as classmates.

*They obviously have a great affection for their home country and a good knowledge of its history: I was aware Romania, the nearest European county I've visited, felt a close connection to Hungary. They explain that Timisoara in Romania used to belong to Hungary so lots of people there would speak Hungarian.*

At the Treaty of Trianon (1920) after the First World War, over 70% of our land was given away. It included ten big cities and access to the sea and a lot of natural resources. We used to be a people of more than 20 million. Now we are less than 8 million.

I had learned English in school. I wanted to move to where English was the main language and to stay in Europe; Monika had chosen German as her second language at school so has learned most of her English since she came out to join me here.

I've started going to an English class on Monday nights [*Monika tells me*] at the Friends Meeting House. I have a younger brother and sister still at school in Hungary. At home people talk a lot about politics – all the time; in a way it is good to get away from that.

*They've been renting a room at Greg's house across the road for two and a half years now. Monika is housekeeper at Greg's hotel just a short walk away. Some of the other tenants work for Greg, but not all. They had asked if I would do the interview on a Sunday evening; both work long hours, they have a little free time then.*

My day starts at 7.45 with breakfast: tables to reset, toast, coffee and tea to serve, orders to take and waitressing to do. When breakfast is over, the team works on the room list till about 3 in the afternoon with a break for lunch at 12. Sometimes I'm asked to do waitressing on a night as well from 6 till 10. It's a good team to work with; there's a Lithuanian girl in charge and another Hungarian girl there and four or five English people.

*Istvan is a plasterer by trade; a craftsman really.*

Plastering is an art form; you create something; it is satisfying especially when you are doing restoration work. Two months ago I decorated a restaurant. It was a nice job. I was self-employed then but I work for a company now, because of the recession. I learnt fancy plastering back home in Hungary. I have in addition learned solid, flat plastering in England. But I take great pride in making beautiful cornices and ceiling roses. In a way, an apprenticeship takes a lifetime. I have a bible; it is a book by a Mr William Millar: *Plastering Plain and Decorative*. He was a Scottish plasterer who worked in London in the nineteenth century. If you have that book you can't go wrong. [*I learn from the internet that Millar's book was first published in 1897 and reissued in 1997.*]

It is not only an interesting historical document, it is a vital record of the skills and knowledge that existed 100 years ago. Much of this knowledge has been lost because of the de-skilling of the building trades and the demise of the apprenticeship system. [*Now there are plans to reintroduce a widespread apprenticeship scheme.*]

*Was York the first place you came to in England, Steve?*

No I started in a dreadful place. You wouldn't want to know about it. There was a lot of trouble – police on the streets most nights sorting out fights, a very mixed ethnic community in the area we lived which was all rented accommodation. There was one terrible incident that stays in my mind: my landlord used to look after a boy from a Barnados home occasionally. He had left me in charge and soon someone was knocking on the door telling me Thomas was on the roof; he was drunk – didn't know where he was. I had to talk him down and pull him in through an upstairs window. It was so stressful. I never want to be in that situation again. It was a dreadful place. It had nothing aesthetic, there was no beautiful architecture there, not like York.

*And the place's name?*

Doncaster.

*I confess this was the town of my birth, though I have no affection for it, it sounds a much-changed place. I remember the river Don being full of the white froth of industrial pollution. Much of its industry, including plant works for the railways, are long since closed as are all the outlying mining communities so its social problems will be greater now.*

We also stayed in Nottingham for a week, that was nearly as bad. It is good here in York. And we love North Yorkshire. We have a car but it is in the garage at the moment for repair. We have been to the Lake District and to the coast – Hungary is land-bound of course. We went to Scotland right up to John o'Groats – so beautiful. I think Scotland is our favourite place. I am a fisherman and my great dream is to catch a salmon. Travelling is so much easier here; the roads are good, the paperwork is easy, you can top up your parking by phone, everything so simple and well organised. Not like home. Once we went by bus to Austria. We were three hours late and thought we would have lost our money – but it was so simple; they put us on the next bus. It only cost £1 to change the booking. At home if you're late, you're late – all would be lost.

*Do you miss home?*

Well, we phone regularly, Monika sometimes four times a week and we have internet; and we have travelled back by car several times. It is a good journey. We can do it in twenty-four hours. But this Easter our parents are coming to visit us here. We are so looking forward to showing them round. But they don't speak English.

We can't imagine going back home to live. A lot of people back home are unemployed. Though we do miss our family. I have a brother and sister too. And we miss a little bit the cuisine as well. We can stay here now we are in the EU as long as we have jobs. We would like to move to a bigger home. To have our own space. We are tired of all the changes of tenants and most of all I could really do with a workshop. But we hope to stay in York. York is such a friendly place.

*Interview 07/03/2010*

*Postscript: Monika and Istvan were married in Hungary in May.*

## Raf
*Polish chef and photographer*

*I haven't met Raf before. We have spoken on the phone and I have heard a little about him from his housemates, Stevo and Monika, and from his landlord Greg. He arrives at my door all smiles and apologies.*

So sorry I had to postpone last week, the restaurant was short-staffed, and I was asked to do a lot of extra hours. It is the nature of the business; we sometimes have to work long hours at short notice to keep things going. And of course the extra money is welcome!

*He has been a chef at Plunketts in Petergate for four years now. This bearded, genial young man has a definite eastern European look. He is in fact Polish – grew up in a village 30 miles outside Wroclaw in the south west near the German/Czech border.*

Mum died when I was 14; she'd had kidney problems for many years. We moved into Wroclaw after that – the fourth biggest city in Poland. I went to high school and did a year of college there; I specialised in European studies. I wanted to come to England to find out about English culture; I had never met English people before.

It was 2004 when I came over, not long after we joined the EU, to get some work experience. I'd anticipated going back to Poland fairly soon. I spent the first six months in Cumbria – loved the Lake District. I worked in bars, kitchens, restaurants. I moved to York in 2005; lived out at Bell's Farm first, but then friends got me this place at Greg's house a couple of years ago. I'd had an accident on holiday in Spain. I'd done about half of the pilgrim route to Santiago; but then the feet, they were destroyed. It was bad. That's when I took up the IT for a bit. So here I am – I still haven't gone home; life is easier here financially and in terms of lifestyle. But I am missing my country. I was saddened to hear of the plane crash back home. [*10/04/10 – 96 Polish politicians, including President Lech Kaczynski lost their lives on the way to Smolensk to mark the anniversary of the tragedy at Katyn.*] A great shame for all their families; for me some of my favourite politicians were on that plane; they were people who knew what they were doing, intelligent people.

You have just got a Conservative-Liberal coalition government. They talk about change, but I do wonder if things will change much – your economy is in such bad shape. Poland was one of the only European countries to have any growth at the end of last year. My politics are much further to the left. There's an election coming up in June and I will be home then supporting the Communist candidate. He's not popular, but I share his views. He's young but getting better and better. It will be difficult for him and I suspect the conservatives will win there too.

I couldn't vote in your election because I haven't applied for dual citizenship. I don't need a British passport to travel. I love travelling; I like to keep moving and see new people and suddenly realise I have been doing the same thing for a long time now. I want to go back to visit South America again, to go to Chile. I was there last January, have a girlfriend there. I really want to spend time exploring rural Chile and do the Ché Guevara route. I'm a keen photographer. I brought back some good photos from my last visit. Normally I'm more interested in landscape, but I took pictures of people there – some wonderful faces – and I made new friends. I might stay there and work for a bit. Greg says he would try to find a place for me here when I come back. Then in another three to five years I will try to get home. Though my father has been living in New York for about five years now and my sister spends a lot of her time there. She works in an office and as a receptionist in a hotel.

I would also really like to develop my hobby, my interest in photography into a job – but that is so hard. I take all sorts of shots, landscapes, buildings, castles, animals. Other people say I'm good at portraits. What I would really like is to sell my work to some magazine. I have a friend who works on a magazine and a teacher who is trying to help. I have had exhibitions – four in Poland, and one at an independent gallery in Leeds. My boss at Plunketts is very encouraging; he says I can have an exhibition in his cocktail bar, and I know owners of pubs and bars who are interested; but of course it takes time to put an exhibition together.

*I told Raf that City Screen and the Theatre Royal both have gallery space and encourage local artists and photographers as does the Blake Head Bookshop on Micklegate. I had just that week been to see an exhibition of photographs of India by Sarah Hardman, a former student, who works for Shared Earth. I ask about his other hobbies. Raf has a T-shirt advertising 'Rock Underground'.*

I really enjoy independent bands – metal but not too heavy. I don't like commercial music. It's the same with films: I hate the American commercial cinema and celebrity films, but have a keen interest in independent films. I find them mostly on the internet. Random Films have a brilliant collection – you can get them on DVDs. My favourite director is a Polish director, Kieslowski; he makes his films in France, often in French; true stories about ordinary people and situations in their lives, perhaps two cousins who haven't met in years trying to resolve old conflicts, or people who have met randomly, talking about their lives. I enjoyed Hal Hartley's *Book of Life*. It's about people's understanding of who Jesus was, how they make sense of the Bible. Of course like ninety per cent of Polish people my own family are Catholic. I no longer practise but my family, they believe, they still go to church. It was one of the first films shot in digital video.

I think I have a good sense of humour; I enjoy *South Park*. Do you know it? I like its sense of humour, a bit satirical, a bit of a cartoon. But I prefer film to television. Another of my favourite directors is Jim Jarmusch.

Look out for his film *Coffee and Cigarettes*. It doesn't have a plot. He just looks at people's conversations, what they talk about, what they are obsessed with. He tends to look at the world from an unusual angle. The only link is the coffee and the cigarettes. It's just a series of short vignettes built on one another to create a cumulative effect.

*Sounds good!*

*Interview 12/05/2010*

## Fran

*Fact finding and food festivals*

*It's the beginning of August. Fran emails to see if there's still chance to be in the book.* I am interested in social history and in particularly the changing patterns of work life in the twenty-first century. But I'll be in the States for most of August. Will early September do? *Yes, I say, ring me when you're back. Her message sounds bright, cheerful and, I guess Home Counties. I'm right about the accent. Fran arrives looking very comfortable in bright green tracksuit bottoms and trainers. With a broad smile she tells me:*

Yes, I moved around quite a bit as a youngster – Buckinghamshire, Essex, Hertfordshire. My parents split up when I was about ten so I now have what I think they call a 'blended' family with step-parents and half-brothers and -sisters. My mother's moved to Ross-on-Wye now and remarried. My dad is in the States; it was them I was visiting last month.

I've had a bit of a tough time this year – I'm only just recovering from a bad bout of shingles that started in February – it was desperate till May but I felt I had to keep on working. One of my current jobs is as an examiner and moderator for one of the big exam boards and we had to set papers earlier in the year. May to July is just frantic with marking and moderating. It's hard because you have to be spot on – it's quite an exact science. There's an emotional side to the job too, dealing with distraught heads of department who are committed to particular students and question the results and you have to explain, the rules are the rules.

I was more than ready for a holiday and so pleased when my American family said, 'Why don't you and your spots come over.'

So I did. Dad's living in Lexington, Kentucky with my step-mum. It's a very picturesque place, famous for horse breeding. I had a week there, then went to see my brother in Washington DC. He works for the government on a military contract as a material scientist; he has to help protect the soldiers by improving the quality of the tanks, so I reckon he has a job for life what with Afghanistan and Iraq.

I didn't come to Yorkshire till the early Nineties. I was desperate for a career change – to get out of banking. I'd begun to see it as unethical, immoral, exploitative…[*She clearly can't find words strong enough to do justice to her feelings.*]

I'd gone straight into private banking from school. Worked in the day, studied at night to qualify as an Associate of the Chartered Institute of Bankers. After fourteen years I had really had enough. I decided to relocate to the north and retrain. I knew my money would go further up here and the pace of life is better. I like the size and compact nature of York, and you can walk round here at one in the morning and still feel safe. It's much more civilised. I had a small house near Rowntree Park to start with, then moved to this one in 1999. I suppose I saw it as an investment for my pension. I have little faith in other pension schemes. Consequently I do spend quite a bit of time trying to keep it in good condition, keep the slates on the roof and maintain the original features. It was built about 1896. I like to furnish it in keeping with the arts and crafts fireplaces.

Sadly it had suffered bomb damage in a raid on York (29 April 1942). A man died here and there were a lot of casualties in the neighbouring streets. There was a feature in the *Evening Press* on the 60th anniversary – I'll bring it for you.

I found a course up here in Information Science and was glad to retrain in something I could enjoy. Of course it's a subject that moves quite rapidly, there are lots of changes and new syllabi, so I try to keep up to date and have a lot of personal resources at home. For one of the exam boards all the candidates are overseas

– Honolulu or India. Their material is scanned in and all the marking done online. Quite a strain on the eyes. You have to work in small concentrated periods. We work in teams which change periodically and I'm managed 'remotely' by a retired headmaster in Hartlepool.

*You said in your letter you work for three different employers? Does that feel a bit precarious?*

No just the opposite. It's a comfort *not* to have all my eggs in one basket. If one aspect fails then you have the other work. I do supply teaching – I used to do it in deprived areas of Leeds which was quite an education in itself – but ten years of that was enough. Even the 20-year-olds working there looked shattered by Friday afternoon!

My other job is as a civil servant – I'm a librarian working two days a week in Sand Hutton at the government's Food and Environmental Research Agency – it used to be called the Cultural Science Lab. I provide specialist scientific online resources. The government is having to cut back so the collection of specialist journals will disappear because they can't afford the space to house them. It's going to become quite rare to handle and browse a physical collection of journals. I suppose the originals will go to the British Library.

Yes, I do have some leisure time left; I belong to quite a few organisations in York. I'm a Friend of the Art Gallery and they put on talks and social evenings. And some of the people I've met there also turn up at Café Scientifique – that's a monthly lecture series at a range of venues in the city where an expert in a specialist field gives an entertaining introduction to a subject in terms a layman can understand. I remember one talking about the science behind everyday things in life such as hair dye. Fascinating!

But above all I'm a really keen cook. I belong to the Slow Food Movement and for three years now I've been involved with York's Food and Drink Festival; it particularly promotes local producers. It's coming up soon, so you might see me and some of the other volunteers I help organise handing out samples for tastings.

*I go and join hundreds of people milling around a whole avenue of marquees in Piccadilly. They're sampling pickles and patés, cheeses and chutneys, pastries and paellas. Some sit and chat in the food tent; others take their samosas or crêpes to sit round the fountain in the mid-September sun. There are also events going on in the Guildhall and the Mansion House. I'm fascinated by the producers' names... there's the Beez Neez and Demi John. (I picked up a leaflet for the Yorkshire Food Company, but their premises in Micklegate are now shut.) I like the look of the Sloemotion Gin. There's definitely a festive feel as the City celebrates the Taste of Yorkshire.*

*I don't see Fran there that day, but the next evening our paths cross as I'm heading down Walmgate to visit my brother. She's looking very smart and very happy, heading home after a session sampling the wares of a chocolatier at Melton's Too.*

*Interview 08/09/2010*

# Mabuhay

*York's Filipino community is born*

**Autumn 2008:** *A Filipino family were spilling out onto the street next door to Tim. Lots of spicy smells were coming from a vast buffet in the back room and I found myself invited in to join a crowd of family and friends celebrating Rosalie's 40th birthday. I took a photograph of her there. I'd often seen her walking her small daughter, Daphne, past my house.*

**December 2010:** *They've moved to a terrace near the hospital — a very different style from North Parade — this is one of York's white-brick terraces and the property looks taller, more rambling. The lady who answers the door is not Rosalie, but I recognise her from the party and she has the same welcoming smile. I show her the photograph and ask about Rosalie.*

**Millie**: We didn't think you would remember us. Yes, this is my friend Rosalie in the photograph two years ago on her birthday. She lives here too. She will be coming down for breakfast shortly. We met at work; we're care assistants in the same residential home for the elderly at Clifton; that's how we became friends. Mulberry Court. It is a good place; good rooms and gardens. They are collecting stories of the residents there. Rosalie often came to visit me in my previous flat in Burton Stone Lane. We saw an advert for a rented house in a local shop — we made a decision — we would rent a bigger house and our families live together. We both grew up in the Philippines. I'm from Manila, Rosalie and her family from Pangasinan. So your street was the first street where our two families lived together. It was six years ago I first came here from Manila. It was very crowded there.

*With a population of well over 1.5 million people in 38.55 square kilometres, Manila is not only the most densely populated city in the Philippines but also in the world. Millie and I discuss a recent TV documentary about Manila's slums. Families packed into tiny makeshift dwellings in impossible situations, slung under bridges. Millie thinks they get a bad press, but I tell her I was struck by the dignity and the personal resourcefulness of the women who care for their families in such conditions keeping them fed and clean and getting the children off to school.*

Lots of people were coming in from the provinces thinking they would find a lot of money, but they were mistaken and had to live in slum conditions. But this is only one side of Manila. There is beautiful countryside at home and we were luckily born and brought up in a much better area of Manila. One of my friends wants me to go and join them in London. But I have had enough of crowded cities. York is good.

I'm a skilled worker; I graduated as midwife in Philippines. I worked for seventeen years as a nursing attendant on a ward that specialised in neurosurgery and plastic surgery, in a large government hospital in Manila. Ward 6. There were fifty-five beds – all ages from newborn to the elderly. Now we just look after the old people.

Here is Mario, my husband, he works there too now. I tell Mario, 'You must get land job. You need to bond with our daughters; you don't know them.' I decided it would be better for us to have life together in the UK. The year 2000 I think had been the boom year for Filipinos coming over to the UK but they were still advertising for skilled workers. I came first, in 2004, and left the girls with my mother and brother for a while. That was hard. I was the only natural child; my parents had married late then after me adopted my brother. It was a myth at home that more children would arrive after an adoption. But it didn't happen. The girls were at private school in Manila. I wanted them to finish that phase of schooling. And it was hard on my widowed mother. There are no benefits in Philippines, no welfare state, though we pay our taxes. Mario says it is corrupt. My mother had a lot of serious health problems soon after I left. Most Filipinos live with large extended families.

**Mario**: My first job abroad was in Saudi Arabia. An employer had come looking for a cook and I worked there for two and a half years before I went to sea. When our first daughter was not much more than a year old I went to work on cruise ships, you know like *Titanic*. [*I understand but say, 'Hopefully not like the* Titanic. *He smiles and nods.*] I started in lowest rank washing dishes and work my way up the ladder and see, here is the book from my last company *Sailaway*. You see here I am. [*A full-colour plate announces him as the Executive Chef. His two daughters stand beside him.*]

At that time Millie had come here to look for work. Many years I had been away at sea. I was only home three months each year – did not really know my daughters. You can see how beautiful these ships were… [*He turns the pages of seductive seascapes and beaches and beautiful vessels, not a bit like the Titanic but by this stage of his career fully rigged Star Clippers.*] Look at all the rigging. People would pay £5,000 a week for a holiday on these and I would prepare banquets. We sailed the Atlantic and Mediterranean and sometimes Asia. I was in Phuket just a month before the tsunami. The guests would reach the islands by a smaller boat and scuba dive and explore.

I felt all my friends were here in Manila – what should I do? But after three years I brought our daughters out and came and joined Millie. Our eldest was nearly 16 then. They had a lot of friends; they were excited but anxious about the move. They complained at first, 'Why you bring us here; it so boring.' Now the eldest is 21. You can see the banners are up from her birthday party and the 'little one' is 16 now. I have a job as chef in the Care home but… maybe when the girls are married I can go back to sea.

*Rosalie joins us with her husband Rami:*

**Rosalie**: Rami and I were childhood sweethearts. My little girl was just 4 when we arrived from the Philippines. She goes to St Wilfred's now. We have moved on together to this larger house near the hospital. Seven of us: myself, Rami and our child; Millie, Mario and their two girls. We've been together for four years altogether. It works for us. I am also a lay minister in the Catholic church. And I'm in a choir in Middlesborough. Three of us travel there together.

**Rami**: I had been chief housekeeper for number 4 person in Government. An important job for many years. I studied fisheries for a while back home. I also worked for the National Bureau of Investigation. Now I am chef at the Park Inn. In addition we do catering for our friends for parties and celebrations. I too am a lay minister. We are a good team here. Our house has become an informal support centre. People come to us needing help. Help with money. Help with jobs. And they always stay for food. I am very excited about our new project; we have created an association for Filipinos in Yorkshire.

*Suddenly everyone is talking animatedly at once.*

'We are busy doing census to find out how many other Filipinos in Yorkshire.'

'We have a basketball league with Scarborough and Malton and Wakefield.'

'We're going to get a programme of activities across Yorkshire. We will start bingo. Bingo is different in the Philippines. There's volleyball too.'

'Rami is chairman. We all have a role.'

**Rami**: We have a hundred per cent support from Canon Michael Ryan for our new Yorkshire Filipino Association. We're planning a Christmas party at Holy Redeemer Church. We have invited someone from York Council and from the Embassy. You must come too. There will be dancing and food. Here are the details in our *Mabuhay Newsletter*.

Mabuhay *is a Tagalog word used to exclaim 'long life'. It's a bit like vive, viva, or cheers used in toasts or to welcome guests, show hospitality.*

*I am enjoying the juiciest pineapple ever. Millie passes me a serviette to mop my notes.*

*Sadly I was unable to attend this celebration but 300 guests enjoyed the party.*

*Interview 16/11/2010*

## Dan, Libby and Josh

*A baby's first Christmas: advising on wealth, advising on debt*

*As I'm greeted in the hallway by Dan, a dark-haired, dark-eyed young man, I hear an unmistakable cry in the background. I realise my arrival has awakened the baby. Libby soon appears with 4-month-old Josh; he's blonde like his mum and sports a blue baby-gro. Very soon he's all smiles and gurgles, very alert and contented. She seems relaxed and comfortable with her baby who gets a feed from his mum while I'm there. At 24 she's quite a young mum. Just as I was. I see one or two 'How To' baby books around.*

I deliberately avoided reading any books about feeding regimes at first. I just wanted to get to know my own baby in my own way. The health visitor calls every so often and I get on with her.

*Josh has a baby gym and a Winnie the Pooh baby bouncer on the floor. Dan tells me Josh's Christmas present was a bouncy chair that hangs from a door. He's already trying to stand up, he adds with a mixture of surprise and pride.*

*They've just spent Christmas doing a tour of relatives in Devon and Essex – lots of grandparents, uncles, aunties and cousins all wanting to see the baby. Libby grew up in Exeter where her father was leader of a local church.*

We lived in the same house till I was about 10, then we moved into a bigger house so that we could care for my grandparents. My sister lives a bit nearer, she's a family support worker in Sheffield. I'm so pleased for her; I've just found out she's expecting her first child next year. It will be good to have two cousins in the same school year. My brother's up in Edinburgh. Dan and I spent a bit of time there when he was doing some work-related training; we loved it.

*There's a beautiful carved plaque on the mantelpiece amongst the*

185

*Christmas cards in light oak with a central image of two hummingbirds with their full names and the date of wedding round the border.* Mum took up carving in an evening class. I think she struggled most with the lettering.

*Libby tells me that she and Dan met as students.*

I didn't know York at all prior to this; I chose York University simply for the course. We met at a Christian Union Meeting and were married in Heslington Church the day after the last day of my last term in 2007. We got back from our honeymoon just in time for my graduation!

*Dan, just a year older, was born in Barking, East London but the family moved out to Billericay, Essex, an easy commute from the City.*

Dad is an architect and all Mum's side of the family are teachers, though she hasn't worked since I was born. Part of me still thinks I would enjoy teaching, though I know how hard it is. I think there would be more job satisfaction. I have a brother who is out in Malawi working for the government as an economist on a development programme which sounds quite interesting. I studied economics and now I commute to Leeds and work for an accountancy firm, KMPG, which is quite close to the station there, so I don't spend too long travelling. It would be good, though, if I could work in York.

Do I like my job?

*He reflects and carefully considers his answer.*

Well… I don't *dis*like it. But I sometimes wonder if what I do is just helping the rich get richer. It would be nicer to do something I believed in. Although I do find parts of my work more satisfying, such as helping smaller companies keep their key staff. That felt more useful. Most of my work is office based, though occasionally meetings are at clients' premises. It's my first day back today after two weeks off and I've already got a headache! So far it's not been too difficult with a young baby. I stored up lots of holiday time and I've occasionally been able to work from home if Libby's been ill or had hospital appointments.

We both belong to an Evangelical Church movement called *New Frontiers* which meets at York St John. Most of Libby's contacts with other mums and so on are through this church group, though we're aware there's a family with a young child and a Labrador just across the road. But Libby's allergic to most animals. We knew Tim, our next-door neighbour, before he moved; he was really friendly, but Libby would have to keep her distance from Haggis. We've met Kath and Jeannie across the road and would have liked to have come to your Christmas social but were busy with the family tour.

*Libby studied politics. She's interested in how society works though social policy wasn't part of her degree course.*

My reading tends to be factual. With fiction at the moment I tend to re-read my childhood favourites: *Anne of Green Gables*, the Narnia books and Tolkien's *Lord of the Rings* for comfort. But I am in the middle of Andrew Marr's *The History of Modern Britain* as well! Not long ago I read *The Politics of Breastfeeding*. It's by Gabrielle Palmer. [*The author has campaigned on the unethical marketing of baby foods and has worked in China and Third World countries.*] It shocked me really. The book also made me determined to persevere with breastfeeding, despite some setbacks. The NHS has this slogan Breast is Best, but they don't actually supply much support. It tends to come from charitable organisations. I've decided to train as a volunteer to help support other mothers who want to breastfeed.

I'm not in paid work just now. My contract with the Citizens Advice Bureau came to an end when I was four months pregnant and I'm not looking for work. Neither of our mums worked when we were young and I really want to be able to focus on Josh. I did enjoy my work with the CAB and might consider doing that sort of work again. I started as a volunteer and did some studying and went on courses. Then, as a general adviser, I ran outreach sessions to improve access to advice.

The most frequent problem people bring is debt. It always

was a key issue, but since the recession we've seen a bigger range of people with problems such as negative equity, and people in difficulties following redundancy or cuts to their working week. It's hard sometimes when you can listen and sympathise with a predicament, but know it's complicated and there's no easy solution to offer and you can see their frustration. Sometimes you can intervene to freeze payments on bank charges and credit card interest, but it doesn't always work, or you can refer people to specialist agencies. You also have to deal with benefit and housing problems, work-related issues and relationship breakdown. Sometimes the issues are interconnected. The most stressful thing of all is when people feel their home is at risk.

Of course you generally need two incomes to get a mortgage, but we decided to have our family first before we became dependent on two incomes. It must be hard to give up an income for a family once you've started. Not many people have the choice. We feel happy to be able to rent this house for now. We moved here in April. We were in a smaller flat in Holgate before, which wasn't suitable for a new baby.

We like it here, though I don't think we know the area around York well yet. When we were at the University there was a lot of socialising on campus so we didn't often come into the city. We enjoy walking, we both like spectator sports. Dan plays football once a week. We got a car three years ago and have enjoyed trips to Beningborough and Castle Howard; we loved it but that's quite an expensive place to go to. I'm getting into a routine with the baby now and try to make sure I get out most days.

I'm going to start taking him swimming in the New Year.

*Josh laughs and kicks his feet in eager anticipation.*

## A Christmas Party
*Old friends and new*

My young Polish neighbour Raf has an idea; he emails it in the middle of the night: he has lived here three years and thinks people are kind and nod and smile, but he doesn't really know them. He wants to organise a communal activity of some sort, perhaps building a snowman; then offer a glass of mulled wine and Christmas pudding in the street so we can all get to know each other a bit better. 'It may sound crazy idea; it may not have happened before?' Raf comes round to have a glass of wine and talk through his idea with James and myself. Given the sub-zero temperatures we think neighbours will chat longer if they come inside for drinks, so I send a progress report and invitations.

Monika and Stevo come round for a drink too. They will miss the party; they will be off to Hungary for Christmas soon, have already put their snow tyres on. They are so looking forward to seeing their family. They are talking about walks in North Yorkshire. My son is telling the story of going up Snowdon in his shirt sleeves and being caught out in a snow storm! I thought his job was about health and safety!

On the day of the party I'm not quite sure who will arrive. I've had apologies from Will with the news of his move. He's working all his spare hours decorating their new house and hopes to be moving soon. I realise that even though I've finished my interviews there are lovely neighbours I barely know. Maya and Ed from two doors down arrive with a huge vat of mulled wine. We've taken in parcels for each other before, but never had time to chat. This young couple both work in the finance sector. Later that evening they're going out to Paulo's Il Paradiso, with other members of a charity group Maya is involved with for a Christmas social. She hasn't been there before. I sing its praises. This small, unpretentious Sardinian restaurant in Walmgate has become a favourite with a group of my friends. We had such a good night out there on my birthday in the autumn we've kept going back.

Jeannie arrives; we've only met once before. She's written two historical novels. A third was drafted, but she has a total horror of keyboards now her fingers are crippled with rheumatoid arthritis. Ann, who has just had her arthritic fingers and toes straightened, an excruciating procedure, goes off to a Christmas concert and returns later. She's looking forward to her trip to India and hopes her feet will be OK.

Jeannie tells us how much she misses Tim, 'such a lovely warm-hearted neighbour. He would come over and open doors for me if I was stuck. We helped each other out with our dogs. I used to have two. One died the same week as my father last summer; such a blow; my two best chaps in the same week. Our family has always had Westie dogs' [*White West Highland Terriers*]. She's very excited. Her son, head of production at Screen Yorkshire, is due to marry at Sinningthwaite Priory early in January. Fran has arrived with a plate of special mince pies – an alternative version topped with sponge mixture. The two of them get involved in a discussion about wedding hats. John, sitting between them, has to confess the only time he wears a hat is if it's too hot when he's fishing.

Vera is here. She knows Jeannie as a former colleague from Queen Margaret's. I tell her about the warm welcome I was given by her neighbour Millie and her friends from the Philippines and how I'm looking forward to meeting her new neighbours with the baby soon.

Dorianne and John come bearing daffodils and wine. I've just seen them on screen at the Theatre Royal! They were extras for a video in Berwick Kaler's pantomime. Shock! Horror! Giant

Chicken has arrived in York! Apparently the extras had to be up at the crack of dawn for the shoot. Peter has arrived with beer. He can't stay long and is in fact whisked off by Sue who comes long enough to explain she has a problem with frozen pipes in her attic. What are Peter's spanners like, she wants to know?

Meanwhile at the other end of the room Raf has met Jo for the first time and the room fills with the sounds of Polish. Jo introduces his daughter Becky. Later she is comparing boots with my friend Neill. He has joined several street events in the past, but I hadn't expected him this time. He had called in to deliver a Christmas card but stays to chat. He quizzes Maya about inheritance tax planning and enjoys meeting Raf and Jo.

Raf leaves looking very happy about the event.

Teresa and Ann stay on with James and myself. Teresa is just beginning to realise retirement could open up new possibilities. I've had a Christmas letter from Christopher, my very first next-door neighbour here, a retired architect. His life has taken exciting new directions since his move to Scotland after his father's death. He has remarried – an artist who works in glass – and has been busy building a studio for her. A second move from Oban to Kilmelford will mean his boat that was moored in Hartlepool when he lived here will be in sight of his house. His new wife is a former crew member who was widowed. His letters always come with lovely ink sketches of his new landscape.

I bump into Jeannie in the New Year on the way to see Penn House on Bootham before its sale. It is rarely open to the public but has been added to York's Residents First Weekend events (anyone with a York Card can get into places of interest in the city free of charge). It has an extensive display of the Rowntree story with wonderful archive photographs and letters. They are re-showing the documentary about Seebohm Rowntree's work about the York of 1901. Joyce is in the front row, her head tilted, listening attentively to this Quaker story. As we leave Jeannie says how good it was to meet so many people at the Christmas party;

'I really took to that bohemian-looking man with the ponytail: what a warm person.' A verdict I share, but have to explain, he's an old flame, and not from York, unlikely to be around much now he has a new love in his life.

Jeannie points out a top flat in St Mary's where her married life began. As a widow she came back from Old Malton to this area of York where her children grew up. The family later lived in a corner house on Sycamore Terrace which is now a hotel. Would this be Elliott's where Carol worked, I wonder? 'How did the wedding go?' I ask Jeannie. She replies, 'My grandchildren behaved impeccably; the fireworks after the ceremony were just spectacular.'

All the talk of weddings at the Christmas do had led Dorianne to think ahead to the Royal Wedding. 'Why don't we have a party to celebrate Will and Kate's wedding in the spring? It would be good to have an excuse to get together again. This has been fun.' A few glances are exchanged. I worry she might be on dangerous ground here. I know she's not addressing a room full of royalists. When her invitations come round for champagne and afternoon tea, on 29 April even Peter accepts, 'as long as beer-drinking, vegetarian republicans can come.' Dorianne paints all her garden chairs deep blue in honour of the occasion and the bunting goes up. I catch Peter with a Union Jack in his pocket!

St Olave's School, formerly Queen Anne's, built by York Architect
WH Brierley ca 1909. Photo © Andy Falconer.

North Parade in snow.

Past St Olave's church into Museum Gardens.

Monika and her Hungarian family by St Mary's Abbey ruins.

The newly refurbished Yorkshire Museum.

A walk along the river.

Dame Judy Dench Walk leads to town or further riverside walks. The Aviva building can be seen beyond Lendal Bridge.

Ducks on the Ouse.

A walk along Bootham seen from the gates of Bootham Park Hospital (top) built by John Carr in 1777.

North Parade in sunshine and storm. From ground level (top) and view from skylight looking towards Queen Anne's.

Whitby – the old town and harbour. Only an hour away.

## Afterthoughts

Andrew Marr in his programme *This Is Britain* on the eve of the 2011 census refers to it as a still photo of a world changing every day. The still photos of people in this street collected here were taken over several months, which has emphasised the way our lives, the city we live in and the world beyond are in a constant state of flux.

2010, the year in which most of the interviews took place, was a year which began and ended in really severe winters, some of the worst on record in York. It was a year that had more than its share of natural and man-made disasters. While I was recording the quiet ebb and flow of life in this city street, our screens were full of other homes turned to matchsticks by tornados, earthquakes, tsunamis, and floods; hard to imagine that the flooded area of Queensland where Kath once lived was as big as France and Germany put together, or that a tsunami even more devastating than the one Greg describes in his memoir would hit Japan where Kirsty and Simon once lived. As volcanoes erupted in Iceland, political protest erupted in Europe and Africa, banks and national economies collapsed. War continued to rage in the Middle East.

The crisis with the Deep Water Horizon oil spill and the nuclear reactors in Japan sharpened the debate about energy and fuel, safety and sustainability. The mining communities of my childhood have gone, and cleaned of the grime of centuries, York Minster glistens; but today's headlines of increased carbon emissions globally lead some to envisage a York submerged as the world heats up, ice-caps melt and sea levels rise. My son's new job dealing with issues of energy conservation and sustainability in the workplace is a mark of our times as firms address new national legislation.

2010 was also an election year. The people in the street reflected a wide range of political opinions and none, just as they reflected a wide range of faiths and none. 100 years ago none of the women in the street would have been able to vote. The men only if they were property owners or paid rent of more than £10. Women's suffrage and the eradication of poverty were the main issues of the day. In 1906 Asquith won landslide victory for the Liberals. Three years later Chancellor David Lloyd George introduced 'A People's Budget', the first in British history with the expressed intent of redistributing wealth:

> *This is a war Budget. It is for raising money to wage implacable warfare against poverty and squalidness. I cannot help hoping and believing that before this generation has passed away, we shall have advanced a great step towards that good time, when poverty, and the wretchedness and human degradation which always follows in its camp, will be as remote to the people of this country as the wolves which once infested its forests.*

This radical and visionary programme was halted by the largely Conservative House of Lords who feared the introduction of a land tax. An election in January 1910 produced a hung parliament which a further election in December failed to resolve.

The central issue of the 2010 election was not individual poverty but national debt. Its indecisive result led to the first coalition government in peacetime for seventy years. Nick Clegg the Lib Dem Leader held the balance of power and despite Gordon Brown's resignation as Labour Leader, Clegg joined the Tories – a surprising coalition given their diametrically opposed policies on the central election issue of the speed and size of national deficit reduction.

This coalition, 'the least legitimate government of modern

Britain', 'one which broke the already tenuous connection between the government and the electorate' (Marquand reviewing Bogdanor, *Guardian Review*, 14/05/11 p.8) left many feeling disenfranchised. There have been protest marches and huge petitions asking the government to rethink its policies on everything from massive cuts in the public sector to its plans to 'shake-up' the NHS. Plans to compel hospitals to compete for patients and income which would destroy key services and betray the National Health Service's founding principle is worrying, not only for the health workers in the street but those of us dependent on its services.

Thanks to improvements in living conditions and the Health Service, a child born in the worst areas of Britain today stands a ten times better chance of surviving their first year than in the best places in Britain a century ago. But there are huge differences still in people's life and health chances in different areas of the country. Social geographer Danny Dorling argues convincingly that we are back to the Edwardian era of great socio-economic injustice; only America, he says, is a more divided country. (See his book *So You Think You Know About Britain?*) Statistics out this spring show a quarter of Yorkshire's children live in poverty. One aspect of this poverty is that these children don't own a single book and a third are not read stories. When Kate Atkinson came back to York Library this year to read from her new novel *Started Early, Took My Dog*, she paid tribute to the vital importance of the library in her early years.

The narrator at the end of Atkinson's first novel *Behind the Scenes at the Museum*, written just before the Millennium, sees York as a fake city:

> *A progression of flats and sets and white cardboard battlements and mediaeval half-timbered house kits that have been cut and glued together. The streets are full of strangers – up-market buskers, school parties and coach parties ... there are no more*

*barbers and bakers or stained-glass makers — it's like one big,*
*incredibly expensive souvenir shop.*

Since my move to this street the Post Office, hardware and fish shop at nearby Clifton Green have gone, as well as Whiting's Deli at Bootham. Meanwhile, Gillygate, one of my former routes to work, the street saved from planning blight by Joyce's boss John Shannon, has seen the growth of many small businesses such as the *Tarts and Titbits* deli where you can find umpteen varieties of freshly baked bread and locally sourced organic vegetables. Many other thriving small businesses here now well established, including my hairdresser Bea at *Cuts* and the prize-winning Café Number 8, give a sense of personal service.

In the ten years since *Behind the Scenes* was published York has been quite a vibrant place. On my regular walks across the city to visit my brother near the Early Music Centre in Walmgate, which hosts both the early and late music festivals, I pass the quirkiest of shops, where you can buy everything from tutus to tattoos; specialist fountain pen shops and antique booksellers jostle with Miniature Worlds of the doll's house. The Hairy Fig, close to York's oldest and smallest pub The Bluebell, is another source of delicious bread. However there are worrying signs; suddenly there are too many closing-down sales. Borders bookshop still stands empty; the Blake Head bookshop and restaurant on Micklegate which I recommended to Raf as a photography and art space is closed; as is the nearby Yorkshire Food Company which I learned about at the Food Festival. The huge proliferation of restaurants and bistros in the city are now competing for a decreasing number of diners.

Sitting in the restaurant this summer at Gray's Court which is attached to the Treasurer's House near the Minster I marvelled that this wonderful building had once been my workplace. It was formerly leased by the college from the National Trust and for many years housed our department. But it was important to me that our students were not predominantly from privileged backgrounds. Students came from alternative routes and access courses; some of the best were mature students financing themselves through a second chance at education. I wonder what chance for similar students today now tuition fees are set to rise as high as £9,000.

York has just been voted the country's best small city; in receiving the prize the Head of the local Tourist Board praised York's citizens for the part their friendliness had played in that award. The city may be full of tourists, but they are real people too, as are those who entertain them. Some of the city's efforts to improve for its tourists have also benefited its residents. And those buskers, whether they're African dance bands or Peruvian pipe players, enliven my day too.

The stories here give a flavour of the dailiness of people's lives but also record landmark events: births and deaths, engagements and weddings, meetings and partings, retirements and new directions; people have moved into and out of the street, into and out of changing states of health, changing states of mind. Our sense of who we are shifts constantly as we cross defining lines, from childhood to young adulthood, from student to worker, from the world of work to retirement.

Whereas a century ago only 100 people reached their 100th birthday, this year there are 12,000 and projections that 1 in 5 will live to be a 100 before the century is out. This is a projection based on past performance, which I treat with some scepticism.

Peter suggested the city has lost its soul with the loss of major employers, but many like Kirsty and Simon still find the workplace provides them with a social group too. The city also has thriving groups who share cultural interests. Choirs practise in halls and churches; folk musicians meet informally in pubs like The Maltings or the Tap and Spile; poets get together regularly at the Exhibition and the Yorkshire Terrier in Stonegate. Script writers try out their work at York's Studio Theatre. There are the

Settlement Players and the Light Opera and Café Scientifique and the Art Workers Guild, many groups which show York has a living culture alongside its historic attractions. York's Open Art studios celebrated its 10th anniversary year this year, offering a wonderful range and variety of artists' work here on our doorstep, including a chance to see a demonstration of stained glass-making. I walked towards the Millennium Bridge which has opened up a circular riverside walk, to visit former tutor Lesley Seeger one of many local artists whose work brightens our hospital in the Art for Hospitals scheme. On the way home I called in at the City Art Gallery to feast my eyes on David Hockney's *Bigger Trees Near Warter* filling a whole wall there.

Having easy access not only to the Wolds of Hockney's paintings but to the dales and moors and coast of rural North Yorkshire is important to many living here.

The process of putting together this collection of stories has been an enriching experience. 2111, a century from now, may well be the last time people will be able to glimpse into the past via census records as I have done this year. The census itself is one of the targets of the current spending review.

When I walk down Bootham now, I am much more aware of the ghost of a past world behind the present facades. I hope this collection arouses a curiosity not only about the historic context of the streets we live in but also the value of neighbourliness and the richness of real people's lives here and in other ordinary streets up and down the country.

# Appendices

## North Parade in the York Blitz

The German bombing raid on York in the early hours of 29 April 1942 was one of the Baedeker raids, reprisal attacks for the devastation of Lubeck, a city of mediaeval, half-timbered houses which had been attacked by RAF bombers the previous month destroying 1,000 dwellings and killing 500 civilians.

The main target in the raid on York when twenty or so bombers flew over the city was the wagon-building works and railway station which was badly damaged; the nearby Bar Convent was badly hit, as was the Guildhall and many other streets especially in this area of the city. A direct hit totally destroyed some houses in Queen Anne's Road. In a photograph from *The York Blitz 1942* a rescue squad and rubble are blocking the entrance to Queen Anne's Road. Fires are still burning here and firemen hosing down the smoking shell of the buildings. To the right, just before the turn into North Parade, houses are little more than rubble. Two died there, six died further down Queen Anne's Road and one in North Parade. Altogether within the city 92 lives were lost that night including 14 children. 9,500 houses were damaged or destroyed. There were no figures for the RAF personnel in the guardroom at Clifton airfield which had taken a direct hit.

The two bombs dropped in the school grounds had left windows twisted and broken, doors torn off their hinges and a chaos of splintered glass and shattered ceilings. Audrey Lee, a student and messenger for the Queen Anne Rest Centre, recalls, 'There were many people about, some who had just arrived with soot on their faces, and most of them dressed very queerly in whatever they had rescued or been given. In the dim flickering light of the hurricane lamps the strangeness of the scene was accentuated.' A Queen Anne Youth Service group had been recently formed and the girls helped in Rest Centres, Civic Restaurants and as messengers for hospital and billeting purposes.

It was York poet Don Walls and his friend who as boys discovered the shells Kath was talking about. They saw strange holes in the mudflats of Clifton Ings. At the bottom of each hole were German incendiary bombs, narrow metal cylinders sporting letters and numbers which the boys took home as war trophies and kept in the garden shed until they were discovered by alarmed parents who called in the Army.

For other wartime memories see:

Van Wilson's oral history book, *Rations, Raids, Romance.*
Leo Kessler and Eric Taylor, *The York Blitz 1942,* The Ebor Press, 1986.
*The Story of a School: Brook Street to Queen Anne 1910-1985,* compiled and edited by Jean F Lloyd.

# Census Details

*Census records for North Parade 1901 and 1911*

## 1 NP

**1901:** Ralph SHIRT (36), a Railway Clerk b. 1865 Pocklington. Wife Caroline (34); sons Arthur (6) Harry (4) b. York

**1911:** Charles ROBINSON (48) Caretaker of a Wesleyan Church. He and wife Katherine (48) were b. Lincolnshire. Sons Samuel (23) a Railway Clerk, Bertie (21) a Miller's Clerk and daughter Elsie (16) all b. York.

## 2 NP

**1901:** Harry BIRCH (38) Ticket Examiner NER b. Escrick. Wife Alice (37) b. Holtby. Daughters: Maud (14) and Leonora (10) b. York. Lodger Hanson JOWETT (24) an Ironmonger b. Halifax.

**1911:** The Birch family is still at 2 NP. Leonora is now a clerk, father an excess inspector for NER; mother a shopkeeper. Maud has gone, as has the lodger.

## 3NP

**1901:** Ralph CURRIE (35) Printer's Overseer b. 1866 Newcastle on Tyne. Wife Mary (37) b. Hartlepool. Daughters: Alice (4) b. Gateshead; Doris (1) b. York.

**1911:** The Curries still at 3 NP with another child, Ralph (6).

## 4 NP

**1901:** Eliza CURTIS (58) Head of household, single, living on her own means b. 1843 Spalding Lincs. Niece Maud CRAMPTON (33) also single, a Miniature Painter b. Farcet Hunts.

**1911:** Fred JOHNSON (42) Elementary School Teacher Assistant b. York. Wife Annie (36) b. Lucknow India. Six children: Cecil (13), Elsie (12), Maysie (9), Dorothy (6), Molly (4), Ronald (2) b. York.

## 5 NP

**1901:** Basil HURWORTH (33) Ale & Porter Merchant's Bookkeeper b. York. Wife Elizabeth (35) b. Leyburn.
**1911:** William HAWKINS, (36) Clerk b. 1875 Huddersfield. Wife Clara, son Cyril (4) and baby Irene b. York.

## 6 NP

**1901:** George KENNEDY (27) Railway Clerk b. 1874 Ripon. Wife Emily (22) b. Stokesley and their daughter Doris (3) b. York.
**1911:** Harry CALVERT, (35) P.O. Sorting Clerk Telegraphist b. 1876 Ferry Hill. Wife Annie (36) and daughter Doris (9) b. York.

## 7 NP

**1901:** Charles ELLISON (37) Railway Clerk and wife Emma (33) both b. York. Sons Charles (9), George (6) daughter Mildred (2). General Service Domestic Sarah BOYNTON (17) b. York.
**1911:** Harry COLMAN (29) Building Contractor b. York. Wife Elizabeth (31) b. Lockton. Married eight years they had one daughter, Vera (1).

## 8 NP

**1901:** Thomas STOREY (32) Railway Clerk Newcastle. Wife Mary (31) b. Cumberland. Daughter Edith (5) b. Gateshead.
**1911:** No entries for this property.

## 9 NP

**1901:** Edward NUTCHEY (33) Railway Clerk b. 1868 Tadcaster. Wife Sara (34) b. Scarborough. Son Edward (4) b. York. General Servant Domestic Ethel GOODRICKE (19) b. Murton Nr York.

**1911:** Arthur LORRAINE (37) Accountant's Clerk b.1874 Manchester. Wife Isabella (36) and daughter Alice (9) b. York.

## 10 NP

**1901:** William STURDY (44) Foreman Railway Porter and wife Lydia both b. 1857 Helmsley. Daughter Charlotte (18) b. York is a Pupil Teacher. **Second Head of household**: James SIMPSON (52) Master Tailor b. York.

**1911:** William ALLEN (32) a Plumber and wife Mary (35) both b. Wandsworth. Daughter Elwyn (3) b. York. Boarder Rebecca WATTS (76) a Widow b. Suffolk (Mary's mother).

## 11 NP

**1901:** Charles HORLAND (29) Auctioneer's Clerk b. Harrow on the Hill, London. Wife Mary (27) b. Lockton Yorks.

**1911:** Same couple. No family.

## 12 NP

**1901:** Elliot STEVENSON (52) Gardener b.1849 Frodingham Nr Driffield. Wife Kate (50) b.1851 Nafferton Yorks. Daughters: Laura (23) Schoolmistress; Twins Ada and Edith (16) a Cashier Grocery Department and Elsie (12) b. York.

**1911:** Edmund TAYLOR (34) Railway Clerk and his wife Elizabeth (30) both b. Hull.

## 13 NP

**1901:** Sarah DEIGHTON, Widow (54). Living on own means b.1847 Sicklinghall. Son John (22) Postman; daughters Edith (24) Tobacconist's Assistant and Isabella (20) Dressmaker b. York.

Fred COATES, Lodger (17) Grocer's Assistant b. Welburn N. Yorks. **2nd Head** Rachel SIMPSON (76) Widow (Sarah's mother) b. 1825 Myton on Swale.

**1911:** Mary DIXON, Boarding House Keeper b. 1868 Lincs. Two Boarders: Arthur JONES (31) Ironmonger's Assistant b Newport; John FRANK (48) Ledger Clerk b. Hutton Le Hole.

## 14 NP

**1901:** Susan GOULTON, Widow (87) b. Hull and Emily WRIGHT (32) Servant, b. Beds.

**1911:** William HESELWOOD (33) Wholesale Druggist's Clerk and wife Edith (33), daughter Hilda (3) all b. York. Boarder Herbert PLACE (28) Ale And Stout Bottler's Clerk b. York.

## 15 NP

**1901:** Teresa DIXON, Head, Widow (69) b. 1832 York; daughter Mary (35) b. Lincolnshire. Thomas CROSSLEY (29) Shirt Cutter b. 1872 Leamington Spa. Charles RICHARDSON (24) Estate Clerk b. Alston Cumberland.

**1911:** Elizabeth WAWNE, Widow (48) Boarding House Keeper b. 1863 York. Boarder John MURPHY (43) Army Pensioner Military Record Clerk, b.1868 Dublin.

## 16 NP

**1901:** Frank TODD (42) Insurance Agent; his wife Louisa (38) both b. York. Daughter Ethel (6) b. Appleton Le Moors.

**1911:** Sarah ROBSON, Head, Single (50). Lets Apartments b.1861 Helmsley. Niece Marian WILSON (32) b. Malton. Boarders Albert WATON (22) Teacher/Social Worker b. Gateshead; Roland DE LITTLE (28) Railway Clerk b. York.

## 17 NP

**1901:** Charles MOSES (42) Inspector Yorkshire Fishery Board; wife Minnie (35) b. Helmsley. Children: William (13), Olive (8), Norman (2) all b. York.

**1911:** George FLINT (30) Married Insurance Clerk b. 1871 York.

## 18 NP

**1901:** John BEHARRELL (28) Clerk Secretary's Office NER b.1873 York; wife Kate (23) b. Sheffield; son George (1) b.York.
**1911:** Alfred IREDALE (31) Commercial Clerk b. Seacroft; wife Jane (31) b.York.

## 19 NP

**1901:** Alice ANDERSON Head, Married (46) b. 1855 Riccall and four Wards: Ethel SPOFFORTH (14); Thomas P SPOFFORTH (12); Olive SPOFFORTH (8); Stanley A SPOFFORTH (2). Boarder Thomas HARWOOD (21) Ironmonger b.York.
**1911:** Thomas MAUDE (56) Railway Clerk b. Scarborough; wife Sarah (52) b. Hull; daughter Ethel (25).

## 20 NP

**1901:** Charles FENBY (32) Elementary School Master b. Scarborough; wife Frances (27) b. Dorsetshire.
**1911:** The Fenbys now have a daughter Frances Mary (7).

## 21 NP

**1901:** Arthur RADCLIFFE (32) Professor Of Music Violinist b. 1869 Elland; his wife Cecilia (30) b.York; their daughter Millicent (3). Elizabeth FARRAR, Widow (65), b. Hackney.
**1911:** Arthur, Cecilia and Millicent Radcliffe still at 21 NP with son Alison George (6).

## 22 NP

**1901:** Oswald BROWN (29) Solicitor b. 1872 Sheffield; Wife Annie (40) b. Darlington; baby son Cuthbert. Eliza BANISTER, Visitor, Married (57) b. Preston. Annie QUIN, Servant (17) b.York.
**1911:** Joseph Thompson NORMAN, 37 Flour Millers Traveller, b. 1874 Holker. Ethel (26) b.York; son Joseph (2) b.York.

**23 NP**

**1901:** John BELL (35) Locomotive Fitter; wife Clara (34) sons Fredrick (14) Telegraph clerk, Charles (13); daughters Gertrude (11), Kathleen (10) all b. York.

**1911:** Lionel MATTHEWMAN (38) Brewer's Clerk b. 1873 Wakefield; wife Mabel (34) b. Leeds. Children: Wilfrid (9), Marjorie (7). Joseph MATTHEWMAN, Father (73) Retired Tutor. Visitor Harry HARDING (7) b. Fulham.

**24 NP**

**1901:** Thomas HAY (34) Commercial Clerk b. Grosmont; wife Grace (33) b. Co. Durham; son Cyril (2).

**1911:** John DALTON (35) Colliery Agent b. 1876 York; wife Charlotte (28) b. York. Boarder William STURDY, Father-In-Law widower (54) Railway Foreman, b Helmsley. Boarder, Lily BEWLAY (29) School Teacher b. York.

**25 NP**

**1901:** Henry SEYMOUR (32) Ironmonger b. 1869 York; wife Lois (24) b. 1877 Cowlam, Yorkshire. Baby daughter Marjorie; Visitor Emily DUGGLEBY (19) Milliner, b. Hull.

**1911:** Thomas WILSON, Widower (58) Master Builder Now Out Of Business; Daughter Mary (28); sons William (26) Clerk In Estate Dept; Reginald (24) Solicitor, all b. Castleford.

**26 NP**

**1901:** Frederick PLUMMER (29) Chocolate & Cocoa Maker b. 1872 Thirsk; wife Jessie (32) b. Berwickshire; Boarder Robert MOOR (25) Bookkeeper In Newspaper Office b. Gateshead.

**1911:** Robert GLEDHILL (32) Clerk b. Tockwith; wife Elizabeth (30) and baby Dorothy b. York.

**27 NP**

**1901:** Richard TYRER (31) Lithographic Artist; wife Grace (31) both b. Stourbridge. Daughter Grace (7) b. Eccles.

**1911:** George POTTER (32) Squadron Sergeant Major Instructor b. 1879 Eastbourne; wife Flora (20) b. Northampton; baby son George Alwyn. Sister-in-law Claudia BOWL (15) b. Northamptonshire.

**28 NP**

**1901:** Joe HARDY (30) Chemist's Assistant b. 1871 Huddersfield; wife Alice (27) Hull. Sons Joe (2) and Charles (0) b. York. Boarder Lilian HOPEWELL (27) Millinery Buyer b. Newark. Servant Nurse Domestic Ada BARNES (14) b. York.

**1911:** Eliza SPOFFORTH, Widow (55) Private Means b.1856 Pitsford, Northants. Daughters Ethel (24); Olive (18) Millinery Apprentice; son Stanley Albinus (12) b. York.

**29 NP**

**1901:** Fred JEFFERSON (35) Locomotive Engine Driver NER b. 1866 Haxby. Wife Emma (35) b. Acaster. Elsie (12); Thomas (9); Fred (6) all b.York.

**1911:** JEFFERSON, Fred and Emma now 45; Elsie (22), Insurance Clerk; Thomas (19) Railway Clerk; Fred (16) Cocoa And Choc Manuf Clerk.

**30 NP**

**1901:** Arthur MORTIMER (30) Hairdresser b. 1871 and his wife Maude (26) b. York.

**1911:** Arthur (40) & Maude (36); Vincent (7); Audrey (3).

## 31 NP

**1901:** William JOHNSON (42) Boiler Maker b.1859 Sandbrutton. Wife Ellin (44) b. Thirsk; Bernard (17) Apprentice Hair Dresser b. Stockton on Tees. Austin (9), Clare (8), Dorothy (6), Stephen (4) all b.York.

**1911:** Francis FITTON (45) Goods Engine Driver b. 1866 Rawmarsh York; wife Mary (48). Niece Louisa GLADDERS (22) Assistant Teacher b. Doncaster.

## 32 NP

**1901:** Thomas MONKHOUSE (37) Saddle & Harness Maker b. 1864 York; Wife Elizabeth (36) b. Medomsby Co. Durham; son Allan (3) b.York. Mother-In-Law Margaret CUTHBERTSON, Widow (78) b. Hexham. Sister-In-Law Sarah CUTHBERTSON (39) b. Medomsby.

**1911:** Frederick HAW (31), Litho Artist And Designer b. Bedale Yorkshire. Wife Annie (25) b. Welborn Yorks.

## 33 NP

**1901:** William CREASER (32) Coal Merchant's Cashier b. Dunnington. Wife Laura (32) b.York

**1911:** George HALLIWELL (31) Civil Engineer b. 1880 York. Wife Jane (26) b. Lilliesley Roxburghshire; son George Fergusson (0) b.York. Visitor Marjory Fergusson PARK (65) b. Pilsehry Perthshire.

## 34 NP

**1901:** Hannah GARTON, Widow (60) Office Cleaner NER b. 1841 Malton. Daughters Hester (34) Dressmaker; Mary (23) b. York. Boarder Frances BURLEY (24) Elementary School Teacher b. Normanton, Yorks.

**1911:** Hester GARTON (43) Dressmaker; sister Mary GARTON (36) Dressmaker. Boarder James HORSLEY (24) Weaver b. Cloughton, Yorks.

**35 NP**

**1901:** Robert TINDALL (45) Railway Signalman b. Norton; wife, Ellen (39) b. 1862 Beverley. Boarder Harry TEBB (26) Bookbinder b.1875, Beverley.

**1911:** Robert and Ellen TINDALL. Boarder Florence WRICKLESS (30) Librarian b.Wellingborough Northants.

**36 NP**

**1901:** John SUNLEY, Gardener Domestic (53) b. 1848 Stonegrave Yorks; wife Mary (51) b. Kirkby Moorside; married daughter Florence HARRISON (26). Sons: John (24) Furniture Upholsterer; Joseph (21) Railway Signal Fitter; Walter (19) Government Ordnance Survey Clerk; Victor (13); Daughters Mabel (16); Kathleen (10) all b.York.

**1911:** John SUNLEY (64) his wife Maria (61) have son Victor (23) a Clerk; and daughter Kathleen (20) still at home.

**37 NP**

**1901:** Henry WARRINGTON (51) Railway Guard b. 1850 Saxton. Wife Rachel (45) b. Ryther Yorks. Sons Ernest (24) Engineman Electrical b. Barkston Yorks; Henry (22) Craneman; Arthur (18) Joiner b. Ulleskelf. Daughters Selina (20); Emily (16) Dressmaker; Edith (10) all b. Ulleskelf. Charlotte (5) b.York. Boarder Arthur COBB (26) Joiner b.York.

**1911:** George SMITH (61) Signal Inspector b. 1850 Melton Mowbray; wife Charlotte (58) b.York. Son Walter (30) Signalman b.York; Daughter Charlotte (26) b. Gascoigne Worth; niece Annie ARMSTRONG (41) Dressmaker b. Huttons Ambo.

**38 NP**

**1901:** Richard AGAR (45) Joiner b. 1856 Stillington; wife Jane (44) b. Sutton on Forest. Son Martin (22) a Tailor and daughter Sarah (19) both b. Sutton on Forest. Daughters Florence (15) a Dressmaker and Nellie (13) b.York.

**1911:** Richard and Jane AGAR have daughters Lizzie (30), Florence (25), Ellen (23) a Whilliner and Lillian (9) at home.

## 39 NP

**1901:** William CHALLENGER, (24) Traveller For Coal & Builder Merchant; wife Florence (18) b. York.

**1911:** William and Florence CHALLENGER, have three children: Gladys (9); Harry (4); Joan (3).

## 40 NP

**1901:** (Two Heads of household) Robert JACKSON, Railway Carriage & Wagon Builder (47) b. 1854 Bassenthwaite. Wife Mary (45) b. York. Boarder Harry BOWLZER (21) Railway Engineer's Clerk b. Rokeby. Mirian SHACKLETON (27) Head Single, Solicitor's Clerk b. Goole.

**1911:** Benjamen CUSSINS (47) Farmer b. 1864 York; wife Rose (45) b. Horbury Yorks. Children: Reginald (10); Dorothy (9); Eric (7); Ronald (6); Evelyn (3) all b. York. Friend Adela SHEPPARD (54) b. Derby.

## 41 NP

**1901:** Hannah HENDERSON, Widow (41) b. 1860 Ganthorpe Yorks. Son Herbert (16) Druggist's Apprentice b. Ganthorpe; daughter Mary (14) and son John (13) b. Terrington Yorks.

**1911:** Emilyetta DALE (43) and Boarder Clara DALE (32) sisters, both Millinery Shop Keepers b. York.

## 42 NP

**1901:** Marmaduke MILNER (52) Railway Locomotive Driver b. 1849 Norton Yorks. Wife Sarah (55) b. Scarborough; their children Florence (19); Marmaduke (16) Hairdresser's Apprentice; Richard (13); Ellen (9) b. York. Mary HORSLEY, Widow (61) (mother-in-law) Monthly Nurse b. Scarborough.

**1911:** Marmaduke MILNER still an Engine Driver, wife Sarah 'assisting in the house', daughter Ellen now 19, a Dressmaker.

## 44 NP

**1901:** James LAWRIE (55) Clerk Of Works Yorks Agricultural Socy b. 1846 Scotland. Wife Isabella (51) b. Invergordon; son James (21) Foreman Carpenter & Joiner b. Berwick on Tweed; daughter, Elizabeth (15) b. Coneysthorpe, Yorks.

**1911:** Thomas TROWSDALE (51) NER Engine Driver b.1860 Leathorne Bridge. Wife Mary (47) b.1864 Beverley; daughters Minnie (23) and Olivia (21) both Dressmakers; Ivy (10). Son, Thomas (16) Smiths Apprentice. All b. York.

*The information above is taken from the 1901 census details for: National Archive Reference: RG number: RG13 Piece: 4436 Folio: 41. Reg. District: York Sub District: Bootham Parish: York Enum. District: 2. Ecclesiastical District: St Olave City/Municipal Borough. For 1911 Ref RG14 piece 28411.*

# Bibliography

*Local History*
Chris Dowell, *The History and Development of York County Hospital,* Ullswater, 2007

Leo Kessler and Eric Taylor, *The York Blitz 1942,* The Ebor Press, 1986

Jean F Lloyd (compiler and editor) *The Story of a School: Brook Street to Queen Anne 1910-1985*

Nikolaus Pevsner and David Neave, *The Buildings of England: Yorkshire:York and the East Riding,* Yale University Press, 2005

W.H. Scott, *The North And East Ridings of Yorkshire At the Opening of the Twentieth Century: Contemporary Biographies, Pikes New Century Series No. 8* W.T. Pike & Co, Brighton, 1903

Carole Smith, *The Almshouses of York,* York 2010

Van Wilson, The Oral History Series. *York Voices; Stonegate Voices; The Walmgate Story; Rations, Raids, Romance*

Tana Wolf, *York Theatre Royal 1744-1994: 250 Years at the Heart of York*

*York: A Survey 1959,* The British Association in York

Sue Adamson, Nareen Ali and Fasil Demash, *Mapping Rapidly Changing Ethnic Populations: A Case Study of York,* Joseph Rowntree Foundation <www.jrf.org.uk> February 2010

<www.imagineyork.co.uk>

<www.historyofyork.org.uk>

*General Interest*
Nick Barratt, *Tracing the History of Your House,* The National Archives, 2006

Vernon Bogdanor, *The Coalition and the Constitution*

Danny Dorling, *So you think you know about Britain?* 2011

Judith Flanders, *The Victorian House: Domestic Life from Childbirth to Deathbed*, Harper, 2004

Mark McCrum and Matthew Sturgis *The 1900 House,* 1999 Channel 4 Books

William Millar, *Plastering: Plain and Decorative*, Batsford, 1897. New edition 1998

Julie Myerson, *Home: The Story of Everyone Who Ever Lived in Our House,* Harper, 2005

Belinda Turffrey, *The Human Cost: How the Lack of Affordable Housing Impacts on All Aspects of Life,* Shelter, March 2010

<http://england.shelter.org.uk/__data/assets/pdf_file/0003/268752/The_Human_Cost>

<www.freewebs.com/yorkshiremain/bentleycolliery.htm>

*Footnote*

Clifford's Tower stands on the site of a horrific massacre of York's Jewish population on 16 March 1190. A large group had taken refuge from a violent mob in the then wooden tower. Rather than perish at the hands of the mob that awaited them outside, many of the Jews took their own lives, others died in the flames, and those who finally surrendered were murdered. The first motte and bailey castle there was built for William the Conqueror in 1068, as part of a campaign to subdue anti-Norman sentiment in the north. In the latter half of the thirteenth century, the keep was rebuilt in stone. It later became known as Clifford's Tower after Roger de Clifford, who was hanged there in 1322.

# Acknowledgements

Firstly thanks to all the neighbours who made this possible. It has been a great privilege to hear their stories.

Thanks also to:-

Hazel Cameron and *Celebrating Place*, *Creative North Yorkshire* for supporting this project.

Joy Cann, archivist from *Explore York* especially for pointing out the surprising pleasures of the dusty bound volumes of 1890's Council Minutes and retrieving plans from a pile of thousands awaiting re-cataloguing.

City of York Libraries, Archives and Local History Department for permission for images © <www.york.gov.uk/archives> <www.imagineyork.co.uk>

Ryedale Folk Museum, Hutton-le-Hole: permission for photographs from the Hayes Collection <www.ryedalefolkmuseum.co.uk>

Neill Clayton for first showing me the 1893 map and for suggesting the title for this book.

Sal Cline and Carole Angier for their encouragement at the pilot stage of this project at Arvon's Lumb Bank, October 2008.

Ian Daley of Route Publications, Pontefract for his interest and encouragement and preparing this book for press.

Harry Chambers, Ann Drysdale, Joanna Heywood, Teresa Killeen, David McAndrew, Jim McCord, for informal feedback and encouragement.

Linda Hoy for her hard work and sound advice as mentor

Janette Ray for loan of books from her rare and out of prints book shop at 8 Bootham.

Stan, Rummana and Vera for the loan of deeds, documents and books.